The Brothers Grimm Cookbook

For Chris, with all my love

Thunder Bay Press
An imprint of Printers Row Publishing Group
9717 Pacific Heights Blvd, San Diego, CA 92121
www.thunderbaybooks.com • mail@thunderbaybooks.com

Printers Row Publishing Group is a division of Readerlink Distribution Services, LLC.
Thunder Bay Press is a registered trademark of Readerlink Distribution Services, LLC.

Correspondence regarding the content of this book should be sent to Thunder Bay
Press, Editorial Department, at the above address. Author and rights inquiries should be
addressed to Pyramid, an imprint of Octopus Publishing Group Ltd., Carmelite House,
50 Victoria Embankment, London, EC4Y 0DZ
www.octopusbooks.co.uk

Thunder Bay Press
Publisher: Peter Norton • Associate Publisher: Ana Parker
Editor: Dan Mansfield
Acquisitions Editor: Kathryn Chipinka Dalby

Produced by Pyramid
Publisher: Lucy Pessell
Editor: Sarah Kennedy • Designer: Hannah Coughlin
Editorial Assistant: Emily Martin
Recipe Development: Jane Birch
Senior Production Controller: Emily Noto

Library of Congress Control Number: 2021953012

ISBN: 978-1-6672-0081-1

Printed in China

26 25 24 23 22 1 2 3 4 5

The Brothers Grimm Cookbook

RECIPES INSPIRED BY FAIRY TALES

Robert Tuesley Anderson

THUNDER BAY
P·R·E·S·S

San Diego, California

Contents

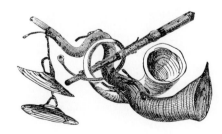

Introduction

The Kinder- und Hausmärchen (*Children's and Household Tales*) by Jacob Ludwig Karl Grimm (1785–1863) and Wilhelm Carl Grimm (1786–1859) was first published in 1812, republished in amended and expanded editions until 1857, and quickly translated into other languages, English included, often in toned-down, not to say bowdlerized versions. The *Tales* crystallized what most of us understand to be a fairy story—a tale of adventure and magic, set in a vaguely medieval, "once upon a time" world, in which a hero or heroine overcomes an evil adversary to make their fortune, marry well, and "live happily ever after."

Such tales had flourished long before the Brothers Grimm—most often circulating in oral form among ordinary people but also captured, at times, as polished literary tales, as in the *Histoires ou contes du temps passé* (1697) of Charles Perrault (1628–1703). The Grimms' versions, however, caught the tales at an important historic moment, retaining many of the more disconcerting elements—the sex, the violence, and the savage black humor—that were subsequently toned down (or jettisoned altogether) for politer, as well as younger, audiences, and which even the brothers themselves tamed through successive editions.

For all their fantastical elements—from magic rings to talking animals, to witches, dwarfs, ogres, and princesses—the Grimms' *Tales* have an earthiness that keep them tethered to the real world. The protagonists are often hungry and poor and, to survive in a hostile world in which everything seems stacked against them, must hone their wits if they are to flourish. Even the rich—the kings, queens, princesses, and merchants—have problems with which we can empathize: difficult family relationships, childlessness, loneliness, fear of getting older, a desire for love and happiness . . . The English novelist Angela Carter (1940–92) captures their nitty-gritty realism thus: "A fairy tale is a story in which one king goes to another king to borrow a cup of sugar."

Carter's "cup of sugar" draws attention to another of the earthier aspects of the Grimms' *Tales* that can easily be overlooked—their preoccupation with food. To some extent, this reflects the very real hunger that existed in the European culture out of which the fairy tales sprang, in which, for millions, famine was an ever-constant threat. "Hansel and Gretel," for one, is all about raw, gnawing hunger. The tale begins with a famine in which a woodsman and his wife must choose between feeding themselves and abandoning (and effectively murdering) their children, and then turns into a surreal food-themed fantasy-cum-horror story in which everything becomes edible, including a house and even the children themselves. Food in such tales is a matter of life and death.

But a more generalized pleasure in food also permeates the Grimms' *Tales*, along with a sense that it is good food shared that helps cement society together. There's nothing fancy or exotic about the food in the fairy tales; it's the plain honest fare that the brothers' contemporaries would have served up at their tables—roast meats and game, cheese, bread, soups and stews, fruit . . . in short, seasonal, simple, nourishing dishes. In the tale "The Wishing-Table, the Gold-Ass, and the Cudgel in the Sack," a magic table that resets itself with a hearty communal meal notably takes precedence over an ass that produces gold out of its mouth and backside. In the world of the fairy tale, good food that can be shared by everyone is both a catalyst and symptom of a flourishing society. That it should be thus in our society, too, is, I hope, something everyone can agree on.

It is this spirit that underpins the collection of Grimms-inspired recipes featured in this book: simple soups, tasty stews, hearty pies, and delicious rib-sticking puddings that can be easily prepared, are relatively cheap to make, and proudly shared with friends and family. *Gesegnete Mahlzeit*—blessed mealtime—as the Germans say.

A Note on Editions

The Grimms' *Tales* have been translated into more than 160 languages, and in the United States alone there are over 120 editions of the stories available to read. The editions used in this cookbook are *Grimms' Fairy Tales*, translated by Edgar Taylor and Marian Edwardes, published by R Meek & Co. in 1876; and *Grimms' Household Stories*, published by Routledge & Sons Ltd in 1853. You may therefore find slight differences in the references to the tales to the version you may be most familiar with, due to variation in translation. These differences are testament to the lasting magic of the tales and their enduring popularity as they are passed down through the ages.

Once Upon a Time

Every sensible hero or heroine knows that you can't set out on an adventure without having a good breakfast first. Whether it's a walk to your granny's to take her some cake and wine ("Little Red Cap") or a trip to the mountains to look for gold (the Seven Dwarves of "Snow-White"), or even just staying put in a tower ("Rapunzel"), a cozy, nourishing breakfast will always get you off to a good start—ready to face whatever the day will throw at you—wolves, warlocks, witches, all.

Historically, too, breakfast was the most important meal of the day, whatever position one takes on its virtues today. A princess might well linger in her canopied, feather-mattress bed until lunchtime, but a working man or woman needed to be up and about at the crack of dawn. Lunch was a rich man's meal, and a farm laborer might at best hope for a bit of bread and cheese tied up in a neckerchief at midday, so getting a generous meal inside them before they left for the day was essential.

Let's take our ancestors' wisdom to heart: begin our day's adventures with a hearty breakfast and we'll overcome every peril . . . as if by magic.

Sensible Elsie's "Good Oatmeal" with Raspberries

"Sensible Elsie" (or, in later editions, "Clever Alice") in the Brothers Grimm tale that bears her name is anything but sensible. She is something of an antiheroine, quite different from the "clever wenches" who, in tale after tale, outsmart their evildoing opponents. She is lazy, easily distracted, and anxious about everything.

In one of the most curious and madly comic scenes in the *Tales*, at her mother's bidding, Elsie goes down to the cellar to fetch beer for a prospective husband, Hans, who has come looking for a clever wife. Elsie, however, fails to come up again after she becomes so worried that a pickaxe left in the wall will fall on her future child that she bursts into uncontrollable tears. One after one, the whole household comes down to see what has happened to Elsie—maid, manservant, mother, father—and they, too, burst into tears at the as-yet-unrealized calamity. Finally, Elsie's suitor goes down to the cellar to investigate and, despite the idiocy of his bride and her family, decides to marry her anyway.

After her marriage, Elsie suffers another crisis, this one rather nightmarish. Told by her husband to go gather corn for bread, she takes a bowl of "good oatmeal" to the field and, instead of setting to work, takes a nap. Hans, discovering her laziness, ties a fowler's net with little bells around her as she sleeps. When she wakes up and sets off home in a daze, the jangling bells unleash in her what can only be described as an existential crisis: is she really Elsie, she wonders, or is she someone else altogether? To resolve this tricky question, on reaching the house, she asks her husband through the door whether Elise is inside. When he replies yes, she comes to the conclusion that she is, indeed, someone else and wanders away from the village, never to be seen again.

Whether it's a cautionary tale of women's powerlessness, marital disharmony or domestic abuse and, perhaps, of ultimate female emancipation, "Sensible Elsie" is typical of the dark, menacing undercurrents that swirl beneath many of the tales.

Super-charge your morning with a simple recipe that's absolutely packed with goodness—protein, fiber, vitamins, and healthy fats all combine in a sustaining breakfast bowl. For a vegan version, use almond milk and replace the honey with maple syrup.

Serves 2

Prep + cook time 35 minutes

2½ cups milk

½ cup plus 1½ tablespoons quinoa

2 tablespoons superfine sugar

½ teaspoon ground cinnamon

1 cup fresh raspberries

2 tablespoons mixed seeds, such as sunflower, linseed, pumpkin, and hemp

2 tablespoons honey

1. Bring the milk to a boil in a small saucepan. Add the quinoa and return to a boil. Reduce the heat to low, cover, and simmer for about 15 minutes until three-quarters of the milk has been absorbed.

2. Stir the sugar and cinnamon into the pan, re-cover, and cook for 8–10 minutes or until almost all the milk has been absorbed and the quinoa is tender.

3. Spoon the mixture into two bowls, then top with the raspberries, sprinkle with the seeds, and drizzle with the honey. Serve immediately.

CLEVER ALICE

And when he was gone, she cooked herself a nice mess of pottage to take with her. As she came to the field, she said to herself, "What shall I do? Shall I cut first, or eat first? Ay, I will eat first!"

Sensible Elsie

Hans's Berry and Coconut Oatmeal

If we have Sensible Elsie's oatmeal (see pages 9–11), we ought by rights to have one for her husband, Hans. Oatmeal has been a staple for hundreds, if not thousands, of years, and all across the globe. In essence, a grain soup, often enriched with butter or fat and bulked up with vegetables, beans, meat, or fish, it was not in origin the breakfast dish we know now but a main meal served up at any time of day. In its thinner form, it was gruel—the unappetizing, undernourishing food of the European poor in the Middle Ages.

The oatmeal here is anything but gruel-like and just the thing Hans, the self-entitled husband of the Grimms' tale, might have spoiled himself with. What are we to make of this man who punishes his wife in such a strange way and then essentially turns her away from the marital home, denying her very identity? Perhaps some earlier readers might have felt that the husband had every right to act as he did—he wanted a clever wife and got a rather lazy, if not downright stupid, one instead—but for us, the sympathies of the tale seem to be all with its rather dozy, ditzy heroine. Let's hope Elsie found a better life—with endless bowls of delicious, thick oatmeal—away from her home village and husband!

Vary the toppings for this creamy oatmeal by trying other berries, such as blackberries, raspberries, or strawberries, or top with roughly chopped dried apricots, dates, or raisins. For a sweet treat, add a dollop of Orchard Fruit Jelly (see page 30) and a sprinkling of flaked almonds.

Serves 4

Prep + cook time 15 minutes

2 cups rolled oats

3 tablespoons unsweetened dried coconut, plus extra to serve

2½ cups milk

2½ cups water

4 tablespoons plain yogurt

1½ cups blueberries

4 tablespoons honey

1. Place the oats and coconut in a saucepan with the milk and measured water. Bring to a boil, then reduce the heat and simmer for about 8 minutes until thick and creamy, stirring often.

2. Pour into four bowls and stir a swirl of the yogurt into each. Top with the berries and a drizzle of honey, then sprinkle with a little extra coconut.

Clever Hans's Sticky Bacon and Onion Pan-fry

Having your wits about you is a must in the world of the fairy tale. Not everyone can be a prince or a princess, and for most of the characters—ordinary working folk—getting what they want—usually a good home, a well-to-do husband/wife, a bevy of children and, above all, a full belly—means pitting your wits against your opponents—kings, witches, and the whole rotten system whose weight bears down on the poor and the marginal. The witless rarely win the day and are punished as a result.

In the story "Clever Hans," Hans fails to use his wits and pays the price. He goes to and fro between his mother's and his lover Gretel's home, bringing back gifts each time that he, in his stupidity, neglects to take care of. The gifts escalate until it's Gretel herself whom he brings home to his mother, but Hans again neglects to look after her, instead leaving her outside attached to a halter to feed on the grass, just as if she were a head of cattle. His mother chides him for his stupidity, and tells him that he ought to be "casting sheep's eyes at her"—that is, looking lovingly at her as his prospective wife. Hans, however, takes her words quite literally—throwing real sheep's eyes into her face, and, understandably, the horrified Gretel runs away.

One of the gifts given en route to this gruesomely funny outcome is a side of bacon, which Hans, instead of putting out of harm's way, drags behind him along the road, where it's soon devoured by the village dogs. Now a really clever Hans would have learned his lesson the first time around and brought the bacon home for his mother's table and this delicious breakfast fry!

This unusual and addictive combination of fried bacon and onion with sweet marmalade is delicious served on thick slices of buttered toast.

Serves 4

Prep + cook time 10 minutes

1 tablespoon olive oil

12 Canadian bacon slices, cut into big pieces

2 onions, thinly sliced

3 tablespoons marmalade

3 tablespoons orange juice

1 teaspoon whole-grain mustard

1 teaspoon thyme leaves

1. Heat the olive oil in a large, heavy-based skillet and cook the bacon and onions over high heat, stirring frequently, for 4 minutes until the bacon is browned and cooked.

2. Meanwhile, mix together the marmalade, orange juice, whole-grain mustard, and thyme leaves. Add to the pan and cook, stirring, for 2 minutes until piping hot.

> *Hans took the bacon, tied it with a rope, and swung it to and fro so that the dogs came and ate it up. When he reached home he held the rope in his hand, but there was nothing on it.*
>
> **Clever Hans**

Little Red-Cap's Oven-baked Sausage Brunch

While there is said to be a cheese for every day of the year in France, in Germany there are, supposedly, enough kinds of sausages for four years—some 1,500 varieties in all. Such figures must always, of course, be taken with a pinch of salt, but there are certainly a wide variety of sausages to be found across Germany's regions—big and small, white and black, curried and herbed, smoked and fermented . . .

Sausages turn up, rather unexpectedly, in the second part of the Grimms' version of "Little Red Riding Hood"—"Little Red-Cap"—one of the best-known fairy tales of all. In this coda to the more familiar tale, the girl and her grandmother encounter a second wolf, but this time around they seem to have learned from their earlier mistakes. Little Red-Cap wisely refuses to leave the woodland path when tempted to by the wolf and instead runs on to her grandmother's house. There, at the old lady's bidding, she pours sausage water into a big stone trough under the eaves (the grandmother has been boiling sausages). The wolf, who cannot resist the fragrant smell of meat, climbs onto the roof but slips down off the eaves and into the trough, where he drowns.

Reason enough to celebrate, you would think. Afterward, perhaps, the triumphant pair might have sat down to a sausage brunch. Poor old Big Bad Wolf!

Savor the luxury of a leisurely brunch with this one-pan pleaser. Add a stack of hot buttered toast, some freshly squeezed orange juice, and a pot of coffee, and tuck in.

Serves 2

Prep + cook time 40 minutes

1 tablespoon sunflower oil

4 pork or vegetarian sausages

2 potatoes, scrubbed and cut into
½-inch cubes

4 mini portobello mushrooms,
trimmed

2 tomatoes, halved

2 large eggs

black pepper

1. Heat the oil in a nonstick ovenproof dish or roasting dish at 400°F, until hot.

2. Add the sausages and potatoes to the hot oil and turn to coat in the oil. Cook in the oven for 10 minutes.

3. Remove the dish from the oven, add the mushrooms and tomatoes, and turn with the sausages and potatoes to coat in the oil. Return to the oven and cook for an additional 10–12 minutes until the potatoes are golden and the sausages are cooked through.

4. Make two separate spaces in the baked mixture and break an egg into each. Return to the oven and cook for an additional 3–4 minutes until the eggs are softly set. Grind over some pepper and serve immediately.

Then the Wolf sniffed the smell of the sausages, and smacked his lips, and wished very much to taste; and at last he stretched his neck too far over, so that he lost his balance, and slipped quite off the roof, right into the great trough beneath.

Little Red-Cap

Eggs

Eggs were an important staple of the peasant families of Europe. Every prosperous household would have kept a poultry yard, with a few hens and geese. In the absence of meat—always a luxury except among the rich—eggs were an important source of protein. No wonder, then, that eggs turn up quite often in the Grimms' *Tales* as well as in many other fairy and folk tales.

However, the meaning of the egg gets rather more complicated and murky in the *Tales*. In "Fitcher's Bird"—a version of the better-known tale "Bluebeard," found in Charles Perrault's *Histoires*, in which a husband kills a succession of wives and conceals their dismembered corpses in a bloody chamber until he is outwitted by his final wife—the egg has a sexual connotation. In the Grimms' still more surreal rendition of the tale, the husband—a warlock in disguise—gives each of his women a key and egg to look after in his absence, and each time the woman cannot resist her curiosity to use the key to look inside a locked chamber. Once inside, she discovers the bloody remains of her predecessors, and the egg she is carrying somehow becomes streaked with blood, which proves impossible to remove. On the warlock's return, he discovers the stain, and slays the wife as a punishment—the bloodstained egg a disturbing image of female infidelity.

At other times, though, an egg is just an egg—as in the comic, fablelike "The Pack of No-good, Low-life Ruffians." Here a cock and hen take a trip into the mountains to eat nuts. To get home they make a carriage out of nutshells and force an unlucky duck to pull it along, with the cock acting as coachman. On the way back, they stop at an inn where they bamboozle the innkeeper into giving them a grand meal and a downy bed for the night in return for the duck and an egg that the hen has laid en route. In the night, however, cock and hen eat the egg and play other tricks on the innkeeper before stealing away before dawn. The tale may be poking fun at the poor who ape the ways of their betters, or perhaps we are meant to root for this barnyard Bonnie and Clyde. Whatever— sometimes an egg is an egg is an egg . . .

Creamy Scrambled Eggs with Chives

Take scrambled eggs from simple to spectacular by adding rich Parmesan and chives and serving them on golden brioche. The key to fluffy scrambled eggs is to cook them over medium heat—any hotter and they'll dry out.

Serves 2

Prep + cook time 15 minutes

2 thick slices of brioche

4 eggs

1 tablespoon butter

2 tablespoons finely grated Parmesan cheese

4 tablespoons crème fraîche

2 tablespoons snipped chives

black pepper

1. Lightly toast the brioche slices under a preheated broiler until just golden, then turn over and lightly toast on the other side. Keep warm.

2. Break the eggs into a saucepan, add 6 tablespoons water and the butter, and beat together. Season generously with pepper.

3. Cook over medium heat, stirring continuously, until just beginning to scramble. Add the Parmesan and continue to cook, stirring and watching carefully, taking care not to overcook the eggs, until the eggs are soft and slightly runny. Remove from the heat when almost cooked and stir in the crème fraîche and chives.

4. Pile onto the warm brioche slices and serve warm.

Fried Eggs with Sage

Earthy and woody sage, fried until crispy and fragrant, pairs beautifully with the other ingredients in this recipe, elevating the humble fried egg to something special for breakfast. Sage has a strong flavor, so a little goes a long way.

Serves 4

Prep + cook time 15 minutes

1 tablespoon olive oil

small handful of sage leaves

1 cup mushrooms, sliced

4 large eggs

salt and black pepper

1. Heat the olive oil in a large skillet over medium heat and add the sage leaves. When they begin to lose color and become crisp at the edges, remove from the pan and drain on paper towels.

2. Add the mushrooms to the pan and cook for 3–5 minutes until just tender. Remove from the pan and set aside. Increase the heat and fry the eggs until the whites are set.

3. Divide the mushrooms between four plates, top each portion with a fried egg, then sprinkle with the toasted sage leaves. Season to taste and serve.

Eggs Benedict

Eggs are a staple ingredient in breakfasts all over the world. Here they are at the core of a breakfast classic. If you want to try homemade hollandaise sauce, follow the first two steps of the recipe on page 21.

Serves 4

Prep + cook time 20 minutes

white vinegar

4 eggs

4 English muffins

4 thick slices of ham

salt and black pepper

1 tablespoon chopped chives, to garnish (optional)

hollandaise sauce, to serve

1. Bring a large saucepan of water to a gentle simmer, add the vinegar, and stir with a large spoon to create a swirl. Carefully break two eggs into the water and cook for 3 minutes. Remove with a slotted spoon and keep warm. Repeat with the remaining eggs.

2. Meanwhile, cut the muffins in half and toast under a preheated broiler. Heat the hollandaise sauce according to the package directions.

3. Place the ham on one half of each muffin. Drain the eggs with a slotted spoon and place on the ham. Season, then pour over some hollandaise sauce and sprinkle with chives, if using. Top with the remaining muffin halves and serve immediately.

Ranch-style Eggs

These spicy, herby eggs pack a flavorful punch and will take your breakfasts to the next level. Serve by itself, or with chunks of warm crusty bread.

Serves 4

Prep + cook time 20 minutes

2 tablespoons olive oil

1 onion, finely sliced

1 red chili, deseeded and finely chopped

1 garlic clove, crushed

1 teaspoon ground cumin

1 teaspoon dried oregano

14-oz. can cherry tomatoes

1 cup roasted red and yellow peppers in oil from a jar, drained and roughly chopped

4 eggs

salt and pepper

4 tablespoons finely chopped fresh cilantro, to garnish

1. Heat the oil in a large skillet and add the onion, chili, garlic, cumin, and oregano.

2. Fry gently for about 5 minutes or until soft, then add the tomatoes and peppers and cook for an additional 5 minutes. If the sauce looks dry, add a splash of water. Season well.

3. Make four hollows in the mixture, break an egg into each, and cover the pan. Cook for 5 minutes or until the eggs are just set.

4. Serve immediately, garnished with chopped cilantro.

The Brothers Grimm Cookbook

Poached Eggs and Spinach

Hollandaise sauce has the reputation of being tricky to make. For chef-level success, the secret is to keep the heat very low so the water is just at a gentle simmer, and don't stop beating. Here it's paired with poached eggs and the green goodness of spinach and asparagus for an all-around health-boosting breakfast.

Serves 4
Prep + cook time 20 minutes

12 asparagus spears, trimmed

2 tablespoons butter, plus extra for buttering

3 cups baby spinach

pinch of freshly grated nutmeg

2 English muffins, halved

1 tablespoon vinegar

4 large eggs

salt and pepper

For the hollandaise sauce

3 egg yolks

1 tablespoon cold water

½ cup butter, softened

large pinch of salt

1 pinch of cayenne pepper

1 teaspoon lemon juice

1 tablespoon light cream

1. First make the hollandaise sauce. Beat the egg yolks and measured water together in the top of a double boiler over simmering water until the mixture is pale.

2. Gradually add the butter, a small amount at a time, and continue beating until the mixture thickens. Add the salt, cayenne pepper, and lemon juice. Stir in the cream and remove from the heat and keep warm.

3. Blanch the asparagus spears in a pan of boiling water for 2–3 minutes, drain, and keep warm.

4. Meanwhile, melt the butter in a large skillet, add the spinach, and stir-fry for 3 minutes or until just wilted. Season with grated nutmeg, salt, and black pepper.

5. Split and toast the muffins, and butter them just before serving.

6. Poach the eggs by bringing a saucepan of lightly salted water to a boil. Add the vinegar and reduce to a gentle simmer. Swirl the water with a fork and crack two of the eggs into the water. Cook for 3–4 minutes, remove carefully with a slotted spoon, and repeat with the remaining two eggs.

7. Top the toasted muffins with some spinach and a poached egg and spoon over the hollandaise. Sprinkle with freshly ground black pepper and serve each egg with three asparagus spears on the side.

There he gave her what she wished, and told her . . . "these are the housekeeping keys, you can look over everything; but into one room which this little key unlocks, I forbid you to enter on pain of death."

He gave her also an egg, saying, "Preserve this carefully for me, and always carry it about with you; for if it be lost, a great misfortune will happen."

The Feather Bird

Pancakes

Pancakes are another archetypal peasant dish cooked since time immemorial. What could be simpler or more delicious than a batter of, say, flour, eggs, and milk, quickly fried up in a pan? Thick or thin, sweet or savory, they make the perfect breakfast dish—delicious bundles of energy for the day ahead.

In the Grimms' *Tales*, pancakes (which are sometimes translated as "sweet cakes") make several appearances. The opening lines of "The Tale of Schlaraffenland" depict the curious image of "a lime tree full of foliage, whereon grew hot pancakes." They appear again in the tale "The Wolf and the Fox," in which the greedy wolf, led by the fox to a country house, cannot resist the freshly cooked batch that they come across while exploring the house for food. In his greed, the wolf seizes and breaks the dish, alerting the peasants living in the house, who "beat him with such a good will that he ran home to the fox, howling, with two lame legs!"

Perhaps the Grimms' most delicious description of pancakes, however, is in the famous story "Hansel and Gretel," in which the wicked witch uses them to lure the abandoned children into her home:

> *"Oh, you dear children, who has brought you here? Do come in, and*
> *stay with me. No harm shall happen to you." She took them both by*
> *the hand, and led them into her little house. Then good food was set*
> *before them, milk and pancakes, with sugar, apples, and nuts. Afterwards*
> *two pretty little beds were covered with clean white linen, and Hansel*
> *and Gretel lay down in them, and thought they were in heaven.*

The pancakes and clean linen represent the polar opposite of the impoverished life Hansel and Gretel have lived as children of a poor woodcutter—unable to sleep because of their hunger pangs and often given not much more to eat than a little piece of bread. The witch's food-laden table—especially those sugary pancakes—must have seemed like heaven indeed.

Dutch Baby Pancake

Also called a German pancake, this is a beautifully billowing and puffy giant pancake. Serve it straight from the oven, cut into wedges and sprinkled with mixed berries, or, for a special treat, with whipped cream and maple syrup. Don't be tempted to open the oven door too early, as it will sink.

Serves 4

Prep + cook time 30 minutes

¾ cup all-purpose flour

2 tablespoons superfine sugar

⅔ cup milk

1 teaspoon vanilla extract

3 large eggs

2 tablespoons unsalted butter

confectioners' sugar, for dusting

1. Preheat the oven to 425°F and put a 10-inch ovenproof skillet on the middle rack to warm while you make the batter. If you can, remove the shelf above as the Dutch baby will puff up.

2. Add the flour, sugar, milk, vanilla, and eggs to a blender and blend until you have a smooth batter. Alternatively, add the flour to a large bowl, make a well in the center, crack in the eggs, then add the milk and vanilla. Use a large whisk to beat the eggs into the milk, slowly incorporating the flour, until you have a smooth batter. Set aside.

3. Remove the skillet from the oven wearing oven gloves and add the butter. Carefully swirl around to melt it and coat the bottom and sides of the pan. Quickly pour in the batter and return the pan to the oven.

4. Bake for 15–20 minutes until puffed up and golden. Remove from the oven, dust with a little confectioners' sugar, and serve immediately with the toppings of your choice.

Mushroom and Herb Pancakes

Making the most of ready-made ingredients, this is an impressive-looking dish for a weekend brunch with friends. The tarragon adds a lovely hint of aniseed to the mushroom and cheese mix. It also works well as a dinner dish with a crisp green salad served alongside.

Serves 4

Prep + cook time 40 minutes

2 tablespoons butter, plus extra for greasing

3⅓ cups baby chestnut mushrooms, sliced

6 scallions, finely sliced

2 garlic cloves, crushed

2¼ cups ready-made fresh four-cheese sauce

6 cups baby spinach leaves

4 tablespoons finely chopped parsley

2 tablespoons finely chopped tarragon

8 ready-made savory pancakes

¾ cup Parmesan cheese, grated

salt and black pepper

1. Heat the butter in a large nonstick skillet, add the mushrooms, scallions, and garlic, and stir-fry over high heat for 6–7 minutes.

2. Stir in half the cheese sauce and heat until just bubbling. Add the spinach and cook for 1 minute until just wilted. Remove from the heat, stir in the chopped herbs, and season.

3. Take one pancake and spoon one-eighth of the filling down the center. Carefully roll up the pancake and put into a shallow, greased gratin dish. Repeat with the remaining pancakes. Drizzle the remaining cheese sauce over the pancakes, sprinkle with the grated Parmesan, and season. Cook under a preheated medium–hot broiler for 3–4 minutes until piping hot and turning golden.

The Fox said he knew a country house where the cook was going that evening to make some pancakes, and thither they went. When they arrived, the Fox sneaked and crept round the house, until he at last discovered where the dish was standing, out of which he took six pancakes, and took them to the Wolf saying, "There is something for you to eat!" and then ran away.

The Wolf and the Fox

Spider's Web Pancakes

Make everyone smile with this lacy, spider's web take on traditional pancakes. They're filled with raspberries and cream, but you can vary the filling to suit what's in the refrigerator: try mixing sliced bananas and maple syrup or blueberries and a sprinkling of ground cinnamon with the whipped cream instead.

Serves 8

Prep + cook time 35 minutes

2 eggs

1⅓ cups all-purpose flour

1 teaspoon superfine sugar

1¼ cups milk

1 tablespoon butter, melted

1¼ cups double cream

1 tablespoon honey

2 cups raspberries

vegetable oil, for frying

confectioners' sugar, for dusting

1. Whisk the eggs, flour, and sugar in a bowl until well combined, then whisk in the milk until you have a smooth batter. Whisk in the melted butter, then set the batter aside.

2. Whip the cream very lightly until just beginning to peak, then fold in the honey and raspberries; chill in the refrigerator while making the pancakes.

3. Heat a few drops of oil in a small nonstick skillet. Transfer the batter to a jug with a narrow spout, and pour a very thin stream of the batter, starting in the center of the pan and continuing in continuous circles around, then across the pan to form a small web pattern about 6 inches in diameter. Cook for about 1 minute until set, then, using a spatula, flip the pancake over and cook the other side for 30 seconds.

4. Repeat to make eight pancakes, stacking them between sheets of nonstick baking paper to keep warm. Serve the warm pancakes filled with a little of the raspberry cream and dusted with confectioners' sugar.

As he entered the forest the same grey old man greeted him, and asked, "Give me a piece of your cake and a draught out of your bottle, for I am hungry and thirsty."

Dummling answered, "I have only a cake baked in the ashes, and a bottle of sour beer; but if they will suit you, let us sit down and eat."

They sat down, and as soon as Dummling took out his cake, lo! it was changed into a nice pancake, and the sour beer had become wine. They ate and drank, and when they had done the little man said, "Because you have a good heart, and have willingly shared what you had, I will make you lucky."

The Golden Goose

Hazelnut and Blueberry Cakes

Often, the Brothers Grimm portray animals with real affection and sympathy, giving the animal heroes of the *Tales* a sparky individuality and charm that can exceed those given to their human protagonists. Often, too, like the best of heroes, they set off on long journeys together, as in "The Town Musicians of Bremen," where a downtrodden donkey, a dog, a cat, and a rooster set off toward the German port city of Bremen with the intention of becoming musicians, but, after a series of adventures, are able to happily set up home together in a cottage. We root for these heroes all the way—as symbols of collaboration and dialogue despite difference and adversity.

Sometimes, however, the Grimms' animals are closer to antiheroes, endowed with all the foibles and absurdities of humans. This is certainly the case with the ragamuffin rooster and hen in "The Pack of No-good, Low-life Ruffians" (see page 16), whose shenanigans during their own flight to freedom show them up as more ridiculous than otherwise. One of the most wonderful, absurd images conjured in all of the *Tales* is of the hen proudly riding in a carriage made of nut shells (the pair have just eaten their fill of nuts up on the mountainside) and drawn by a duck.

The duck gets harnessed to the carriage because she has dared complain that the hen and rooster were eating all the nuts. We would probably agree that they might have been put to better, culinary, use—perhaps in these gorgeous blueberry cakes topped with a smattering of hazelnuts.

Studded with juicy, plump blueberries and topped with crunchy chopped hazelnuts, these light-as-you-like little cakes are a real breakfast or mid-morning treat. They are best eaten on the day they are made.

Makes 12

Prep + cook time 40 minutes

3 eggs

⅔ cup crème fraîche

¾ cup superfine sugar

½ cup finely ground hazelnuts

1⅓ cups all-purpose flour

1½ teaspoons baking powder

¾ cup fresh blueberries

1 tablespoon hazelnuts, roughly chopped

sifted confectioners' sugar, for dusting

1. Put the eggs, crème fraîche, and sugar in a mixing bowl and whisk together until smooth. Add the ground hazelnuts, flour, and baking powder and mix together.

2. Spoon the mixture into paper cake cases arranged in a 12-hole muffin pan and divide the blueberries evenly among them, pressing lightly into the mixture. Sprinkle with chopped hazelnuts.

3. Bake at 350°F for about 20 minutes until well risen and golden. Dust the tops with a little sifted confectioners' sugar and leave to cool in the pan.

About midnight the maiden crept out from under the bushes and again ate with her mouth a pear off the tree, while the angel clothed in white stood by her.

The Girl with No Hands

Orchard Fruit Jelly

The Grimms' *Tales*, despite—or perhaps because of—their disturbing violence and disjointed oddness, can often feel almost hallucinatory—a bit trippy. This is certainly the case with one of the longer of the tales, "The Girl with No Hands." The plot is a complex one, a quilted patchwork of fairy-tale tropes, but it's essentially a love story between a miller's daughter—the handless girl of the title—and a king, and the trials and separations they must go through before reaching their "happily ever after."

In one scene, the girl—who has gone into voluntary exile from her childhood home and who has walked all day—comes, by moonlight, to a royal orchard of pear trees. By now she is desperately hungry but cannot reach the orchard because it is protected by a moat. She kneels to pray for help and an angel clothed in white appears, who promptly empties the moat. Our heroine is now able to enter the orchard and there eat a single pear from a tree using only her mouth. A gardener witnesses her theft, and the following night, when the girl comes to eat another pear, the king, too, comes to spy on her and promptly falls in love.

This rich-tasting jelly captures something of the magic and vividness that occurred in the orchard in this strangest of strange tales.

This delicious jelly makes the most of fall fruit. Try it slathered on freshly baked bread (see page 42) or use to fill the pretty little Linzer Cookies on page 152.

Makes 5 jars

Prep + cook time 1 hour

2¾ cups plums, halved and stoned

2 cups pears, quartered, cored, peeled, and diced

3 cups cooking apples, quartered, cored, peeled, and diced

1¼ cups water

6¾ cups granulated sugar, warmed

1. Add the fruit to a large saucepan with the measured water. Cover and cook gently for 20 minutes, stirring from time to time, until the fruit is just beginning to soften.

2. Pour the sugar into the pan and heat gently, stirring from time to time, until dissolved. Bring to a boil, then boil rapidly until setting point is reached, about 20–25 minutes.

3. To test if the jelly has reached setting point, drop a teaspoonful onto a saucer that's been chilled in the refrigerator or freezer. The jelly will quickly cool to room temperature. Push it gently with your finger—the skin will wrinkle if it's ready. If it's not, return the jelly to the heat and boil it again and retest.

4. Skim off any scum that has formed on the surface with a slotted spoon if needed.

5. Ladle into warm, dry, sterilized jars, filling to the very top. Put the lids on, label, and leave to cool.

The Miller's Wife's Herbed Apple Compote

The miller is a stock figure in European folk tales. While he might often be highly regarded as the provider of the flour needed to make villagers' daily bread, he was also just as easily mistrusted because he could sell adulterated, moldy, or otherwise poor-quality flour, or simply sell it at inflated prices. Traditionally, the miller was considered as greedy, self-interested, and dishonest—in short, not much better than a thief.

No surprise, then, to find that the miller father in "The Girl with No Hands" (see page 30) gets himself into hot water because of his greed. At the beginning of the tale, the miller, while out and about fetching wood, comes across the devil in disguise, who promises him wealth if he gives him whatever is standing behind his mill. This the miller takes to be the great old apple tree that grows in his backyard, so he readily agrees. On his return to the mill, where the cupboards and closets are suddenly brimming and where he tells his wife about his bargain, she tells him that it was in fact his beautiful daughter who was behind the mill at the time, dutifully sweeping out the yard. And so the miller's and his daughter's troubles begin . . .

The sensible miller's wife may well have looked at the apple tree in a very different light after this event—though, excellent housekeeper as she no doubt was, she would have made sure to use up the fall's harvest of apples, perhaps in a compote just like this!

The distinctive notes of rosemary and sage ramp up this apple compote to something extra-special. It's delicious served warm dolloped onto oatmeal (see page 12) or as a filling for pancakes (see page 26).

Serves 4

Prep + cook time 40 minutes

8 Granny Smith apples, cored and cut into chunks

2 Pink Lady apples, cored and cut into chunks

3 rosemary leaves

⅓ cup water

2 tablespoons maple syrup

1 teaspoon ground cinnamon

1 tablespoon chopped sage

1. Place the apples, rosemary, and measured water in a large, heavy-based saucepan and bring to a boil. Reduce the heat, cover, and simmer for about 15–20 minutes or until the apples are just beginning to break down into the liquid.

2. Place half the mixture in a blender and blitz until smooth. Return to the pan and stir in the maple syrup, cinnamon, and sage. Cook for an additional 2–3 minutes, then serve warm or cold.

Magic Pear and Walnut Squares

In myth and folklore, oil-rich walnuts were considered the king of nuts—in ancient Persia they were reserved for the royal table, in Roman legend they were a food of the gods, associated with Jupiter, while the Byzantines knew them as the "royal nut."

In this light, perhaps, it is less of a surprise that they turn up in the Grimms' tale "The Two Kings' Children." The tale is a long-drawn-out romance in which the lovers—a prince and a princess—have to overcome a succession of trials and tribulations in order to be together. Toward the end of the tale, the prince is about to be forced into marrying an unknown bride. However, on the wedding day the princess cracks open one of the walnuts, producing the most beautiful gown. The bride-to-be refuses to go through with the marriage unless she can have the gown and, by devious means, manages to get hold of it. The second walnut, however, produces a still more beautiful gown, but once again the bride manages to take possession of it. The last walnut cracks open to reveal the most splendid gown of all, the wicked bride is defeated and sent away in ignominy, and the princess wears the gown to her own wedding, united with her prince at last.

Here is something else to do with the royal walnut—not half as complicated, but just as magical!

Sure to become a family favorite, this super-easy treat takes just 10 minutes to prep. For a light and fluffy result, take care not to overmix the batter. The squares can be stored in an airtight container for up to four days.

Makes 12

Prep + cook time 40 minutes

⅔ cup butter, softened, plus extra for greasing

¾ cup light brown sugar

¾ cup rolled oats

2 eggs, lightly beaten

1¾ cups self-rising flour

3 pears, cored and finely chopped

1 teaspoon ground cinnamon

1 teaspoon ground ginger

⅔ cup walnut pieces, roughly chopped

1. Place the butter and sugar in a large bowl and beat until light and fluffy. Add the oats, eggs, and flour and beat again until smooth. Add the pears, cinnamon, ginger, and walnuts and stir until just mixed.

2. Spread the mixture over the base of a greased 12 x 9-inch baking pan and bake at 350°F for 30 minutes or until golden and risen. Allow to cool before cutting into 12 squares.

. . . she gave her daughter three walnuts, and said, "With these you can help yourself if you are in necessity."

The Two Kings' Children

In the Fairy-Tale Kitchen

In the Grimms' *Tales*, the vast dark forest represents the otherworld to the daily communal life of the heroes and heroines, the workaday life in the home, the village, or the palace. The forest—which had long loomed large in the Germanic imagination—is a place of wonder and peril in which the characters are abandoned, exiled, or become lost, and where they must face up to their adversaries and be transformed in the process—from child to adult, from maiden to wife, from hobbledehoy to hero, from human to animal and back again. Hansel, Gretel, Little Red-Cap, Snow-White . . . all enter the forest as innocent children but come out of it as young adults, still good but a little wiser to the world.

At the opposite end of this fairy-tale spatial spectrum is the kitchen, the very heart of the home—a place, in the best of all possible worlds, of warmth, love, and safety. It is the space, too, of nourishment, signaling the presence of the mother, even if she is physically no longer there (in many tales the mother dies before or shortly after the narrative begins). After her daily grind of chores, Aschenputtel (the German Cinderella) sleeps by the kitchen hearth, among the ashes, not simply because of her lowly status in the household after her father's remarriage, but because there she is closest to her dead mother. Warmed by the dying embers of the hearth each night, she feels nurtured and comforted.

It is no coincidence that the hearth, the oven/stove, the cooking pot, and the table all recur so regularly, even obsessively, in the Grimms' fairy tales. As we have seen (see pages 7 and 22), the magical cooking pot and magical table that are capable of producing endless plenty are recurrent motifs in the tales—a fantasy of plenty on one level, but also a cipher for the nourishing, all-loving mother. It might be not too much to say that the cooking pot—long a traditional and mythological symbol of female life-giving power—is, together with the spinning wheel (another powerful female symbol), one of the two key motifs of the *Tales*. While we may likely balk at the highly gendered symbolism of the Grimms' stories, it reflected the reigning norms of eighteenth- and nineteenth-century Europe, in which women were largely confined to and associated with the domestic, maternal sphere.

It is this sanctification of the kitchen, and, by extension, the mother, in the Grimms' fairy-tale world that can make its perversion in "Hansel and Gretel" so disturbing and potent for the reader. Here the kitchen is located deep within the dark, dangerous forest itself and upends all the comforting tropes associated with this homely space. Initially, the witch—the inverted mother—lays the kitchen table with a delicious meal, but it soon becomes clear that the oven's primary purpose is not to rustle up delicious stews and cakes but to murder and cook children. While Hans is fattened in a cage and readied for eating like a goose, Gretel is starved—so that nourishment itself has been subverted for the witch's evil ends. Psychoanalytic readings of "Hansel and Gretel" abound: it is hard not to read Gretel's dispatch of the witch by pushing her into the oven as her own usurpation and reestablishment of the "natural" maternal role. Gretel, we imagine, will be an excellent cook!

Bread
& Butter

Every fairy tale has its essential "bread and butter" ingredients. There must be at least one hero—a princess, perhaps, or a miller's son, or maybe even an animal—and usually an antagonist for them to pit themselves against—most often a witch or a stepmother or a tyrannical king or a wolf. There must also be, of course, that classic narrative triad of a beginning, middle, and end—encompassing the hero's journey from "once upon a time" to, with any luck, "happily ever after." En route, magic is not essential, but it helps. It's the wonderful seasoning.

Within this very broad setup, hundreds, if not thousands, of variations are possible, as the Grimms' Tales show, even if just a handful of classic tropes are often discernible—good but poor girl marries well; boy seeks and finds his fortune; children are abandoned but are eventually reunited with (at least some of) their family . . .

Recipes are stories, too—with their own ingredients, their own alchemy, their own happy endings (again, we hope!). Countless variations are possible, but a relatively small number of basics often lie at their foundation. In this section, then, we explore just a few staple ingredients and the recipes derived from them: bread, milk and butter, and stock.

Stocks and Gravies

In the peasant cultures out of which the Grimms' *Tales* in some degree emerged, nothing was ever wasted. Food was precious, and vegetable peelings, the bones from a roast, and any other kind of scraps were retained as treasures, swiftly to be used as contributions to a stock, broth, soup, or stew—the foundations of a following meal. This, however, was not just a matter of necessity or economy, or even of nutritiousness, but of downright deliciousness. Every good cook knows that a soup is made even better by the quality of the stock, which adds a depth of flavor that the fresh, "lead" ingredients alone cannot provide. Much the same applies to sauces and gravies. These very words—stock, gravy, sauce—seem to have a lip-smacking yumminess encoded into their phonetic DNA.

The deliciousness added by the "scrappy" component of a meal comes across in the Grimms' folk-tale-cum-parable "The Mouse, the Bird and the Sausage," in which three unlikely friends—the protagonists of the title—happily share a household. While the bird goes out to collect firewood, the mouse does the housework and the sausage takes care of the cooking. Just before they all sit down to eat in the evening, the sausage slithers through the soup or porridge, imparting just the right salty, greasy, umami notes that the dish needs.

Sadly for our heroes, the story does not end happily. When the bird becomes dissatisfied with its lot, the friends all agree to swap roles . . . The sausage goes out to collect wood and is carried off by a dog; the bird does the housework and ends up drowning in a pail of water, and the mouse attempts to slither through the soup, only to become scalded and die. Now that, admittedly, wouldn't make a good meal. Not every scrap is a treasure.

Chicken Stock

*A duck, pheasant, or turkey carcass or a
ham knuckle can also be made into stock in
just the same way as below. If you have a
turkey carcass, double up the vegetable and
water quantities specified below.*

Makes about 4 cups

Prep + cook time 2½ hours

1 leftover cooked chicken carcass

1 onion, quartered

2 carrots, thickly sliced

2 celery stalks, thickly sliced

1 bay leaf or 1 small bunch of mixed herbs

½ teaspoon roughly crushed black peppercorns

¼ teaspoon salt

10 cups cold water

1. Put the chicken carcass and vegetables into a
   large saucepan. Add the herbs, peppercorns,
   and salt, pour over the measured water, and
   bring slowly just to a boil. Skim off any scum
   with a slotted spoon. Reduce the heat, half-
   cover, and simmer gently for 2–2½ hours
   until the liquid has reduced by about half.

2. Strain through a large strainer into a jug and
   leave to cool. Remove any chicken pieces
   still on the carcass, pick out the meat pieces
   from the strainer and reserve for making
   chicken soup, but discard the vegetables.
   Cover and chill the stock in the refrigerator
   for several hours or overnight. Skim any fat
   off the surface, re-cover, and store in the
   refrigerator for up to three days.

3. If you have a chicken carcass but don't have
   time to make it into stock right away, you
   can freeze it for up to three months closely
   wrapped in plastic wrap, then packed into a
   plastic bag. Defrost it at room temperature,
   then make stock as above.

Fish Stock

*Homemade stock adds a wonderful depth of
flavor to fish dishes, and making your own
stock is a sustainable and satisfying way of
using every part of the fish. It pays to make
a big batch to freeze in handy portions.*

Makes about 4 cups

Prep + cook time 1 hour

10 cups fish trimmings, such as heads, backbones,
   tails, skins, and shrimp shells

1 onion, quartered

2 green leek tops, sliced

2 carrots, thickly sliced

a few thyme sprigs

1 bay leaf

a few parsley stems

½ teaspoon roughly crushed white peppercorns

¼ teaspoon salt

6 cups cold water

1⅓ cups dry white wine or extra water

1. Put the fish trimmings in a large strainer,
   rinse with cold water, drain, and then put
   them into a large saucepan with all the
   remaining ingredients. Bring slowly just to
   a boil and skim off any scum with a slotted
   spoon.

2. Reduce the heat, cover, and simmer for
   30 minutes. Strain through a large strainer,
   return the stock to the pan, and then simmer
   it, uncovered, for about 15 minutes until
   reduced by half. Leave to cool, then cover
   and store in the refrigerator for up to three
   days.

3. If you are adding fish heads, don't cook them
   for longer than 30 minutes before straining
   or they will add a bitter taste.

Sausage Gravy

A Southern speciality, this rib-sticking breakfast treat is great on a chilly winter morning served over hot biscuits, fried potatoes, or hash browns. It's quick to prepare, but to get ahead, make it the night before so all you have to do in the morning is gently reheat it.

Serves 4

Prep + cook time 15 minutes

5 cups ground pork sausage
2 tablespoons all-purpose flour
2 cups milk
pinch of garlic flakes or cayenne pepper (optional)
salt and black pepper

1. Heat a large skillet over medium heat and add the sausage. Break it up with a wooden spoon and cook for 8–10 minutes, stirring frequently, until well browned.

2. Stir in the flour and cook, stirring constantly, for 1 minute. Gradually add the milk, stirring constantly until the mixture comes to a boil and thickens. Keep stirring to ensure the mixture is smooth.

3. Reduce the temperature and simmer gently for 2 minutes. Add the garlic flakes or cayenne pepper, if using, and season well with salt and pepper. Serve immediately.

Beer and Onion Gravy

Give the onions plenty of time to fry gently in the butter so their flavor will be sweet and mellow. If you don't want to use beer, simply replace it with more stock, although beer gives the sauce a lovely flavor and tang.

Serves 4

Prep + cook time 30 minutes

2 tablespoons butter
1 tablespoon vegetable oil
several sprigs of thyme
8 sage leaves, shredded
4⅓ cups onions, chopped
1 teaspoon superfine sugar
2 garlic cloves, crushed
1 tablespoon all-purpose flour
⅔ cup beef, vegetable, or chicken stock (see opposite)
1⅓ cups beer
salt and black pepper

1. Melt the butter with the oil in a heavy-based skillet. Pull the thyme leaves from the stalks and add them to the pan with the sage, onions, and sugar.

2. Cover the pan and cook very gently for about 15 minutes until the onions are very tender and lightly colored, stirring frequently.

3. Add the garlic and raise the temperature. Fry the mixture, uncovered, for 3 minutes or until deep golden. Add the flour and cook, stirring, for 1 minute.

4. Add the stock, beer, and a little salt and pepper. Bring to a boil, then reduce the heat and cook gently for 5 minutes until the sauce is glossy and slightly thickened. Season to taste with salt and pepper and serve hot.

Bread

For the Grimms' contemporaries, bread was the most basic necessity of life. Meat, fish, and vegetables might be essentials, too, but bread was the foundation on which the European and Mediterranean diets were built. Without bread, or without the grain to make the bread, there was hunger and unrest, and the whole fabric of society was undermined. The threat of famine, due to poor harvests and/or the disruption of war, was an ever-present reality: the 1770–71 Great Famine in the Czech lands, caused primarily by crop disease, had killed as many as half a million people, and memories of such catastrophes loomed large in the eighteenth- and nineteenth-century social and political landscape. The symbolic resonance of bread—as the biblical "staff of life"—and its key role in the Christian ritual of Communion—only deepened the power of this simple, nourishing foodstuff.

The Grimms' *Tales* repeatedly bear witness to the importance of bread and its meanings, but nowhere more clearly than in "God's Food"—one of the ten "Children's Legends" appended to the second (1819) edition of the *Tales*. In this tale, a poor woman goes to her rich sister to ask for bread for her starving children, but is coldly sent away empty-handed. The rich woman's husband returns home and slices a loaf of bread, but it oozes blood (what more potent symbol of bread as the staff of life!). The wife tells her husband about her sister's visit, and the husband immediately tries to resolve the situation by visiting his sister-in-law, but it is too late— her children are already dead or dying.

It's a bleak enough parable—but behind its Christian message promoting charity was surely a political one, too: bread must be shared, or woe betide us all. The recipes in this section should certainly help you spread the good message!

Brioche

Enriched with butter and eggs, this rich, fluffy loaf is a real treat slathered with preserves, and you can use any left over for French toast. When you leave the dough to rise in a warm place, take care that it's not too hot, otherwise the butter will begin to melt and make the dough too soft.

Makes 1 loaf

Prep + cook time 1 hour, plus proofing time

4¼ cups all-purpose flour, plus extra for dusting

1 tablespoon superfine sugar

1 teaspoon salt

2¼ teaspoons active dry yeast

¾ cup lukewarm milk

4 eggs, beaten

½ cup plus 3 tablespoons unsalted butter, cubed and softened, plus extra for greasing

1 egg yolk, beaten, to glaze

1. Put the flour in a bowl of a stand mixer with a dough hook. Add the sugar and salt to one side and the yeast to the other. Mix each side into the flour with your hands, then mix it all together with the dough hook.

2. Mix the warm milk into the flour mix until combined. With the dough hook on medium, gradually add the eggs and mix for 10 minutes.

3. Gradually add the cubed butter, piece by piece, and mix for an additional 5 minutes, scraping down the sides of the bowl to ensure the butter is thoroughly mixed in. The dough should feel soft but not too sticky.

4. Scrape the dough into a large bowl, cover with a clean dish towel, and leave somewhere warm for 1½ hours or until doubled in size. Once risen, place in the refrigerator for 1 hour.

5. Remove the dough from the refrigerator and knead lightly on a lightly floured surface for 2–3 minutes to knock back the air. Place the kneaded dough into a greased and lined 6-cup loaf pan, smooth side up. Cover with plastic wrap and leave in a warm place for about 30 minutes to rise until doubled in size again.

6. Using a pastry brush, lightly glaze the dough with the beaten egg yolk. Bake at 350°F for 30–35 minutes until risen and golden. Leave to cool in the pan for 10 minutes before turning out onto a wire rack to cool completely.

Simple White Loaf

Fill the kitchen with the delicious aroma of freshly baked bread. Master this easy loaf and you'll be well on your way to becoming an expert bread baker. Equally lovely warm from the oven or toasted, it will keep for up to three days and freeze for one month.

Makes 1 loaf

Prep + cook time 1 hour, plus proofing time

4½ cups all-purpose flour, plus extra for dusting and sprinkling

1¼ teaspoons active dry yeast

1 teaspoon salt

2 teaspoons superfine sugar

1 cup lukewarm water

1. Put the flour, yeast, salt, and sugar in a bowl and make a well in the middle and pour in the measured water. Mix well with a wooden spoon until well combined. If the dough seems a little stiff, add 1–2 tablespoons water.

2. Tip the dough out onto a lightly floured surface and knead for about 10 minutes until smooth. Then place the dough in a lightly oiled bowl and cover with plastic wrap. Leave somewhere warm to rise until doubled in size.

3. Tip the dough out onto a lightly floured surface and knock back by pushing the air out. Put the dough into a greased and lined 4-cup loaf pan, smooth side down. Cover with a clean dish towel and leave for 30 minutes until risen again.

4. Dust the bread with some extra flour and bake at 425°F for 25–30 minutes or until golden brown and the loaf sounds hollow when tapped underneath. Leave to cool in the pan for 10 minutes, then turn out onto a wire rack to cool completely.

Easy Cornbread

This gently spiced cornbread is just begging for a bowl of thick stew or chili to eat alongside it. Or you could enjoy as part of a lighter meal with the salads on pages 57 and 60. Double up the quantity of chili flakes for more heat.

Serves 4

Prep + cook time 40 minutes

1 cup cornmeal

1 cup all-purpose flour

1 teaspoon salt

2 teaspoons baking powder

½ teaspoon ground cumin

½ teaspoon dried chili flakes

1 egg

¾ cup milk

1. Mix the cornmeal, flour, salt, baking powder, ground cumin, and chili flakes in a bowl. Beat the egg and milk together in a jug and add to the bowl. Mix gently until just combined (do not overmix).

2. Turn into a greased 2½-cup loaf pan. Bake at 375°F for 30 minutes until firm to the touch.

3. Serve warm or transfer to a wire rack to cool.

Rye and Caraway Bread

*The addition of vitamin C strengthens the gluten in the flour, making the loaf rise better,
and the whole-wheat flour, combined with the caraway seeds, gives the loaf a lovely crunch.
You can omit the caraway seeds, if you prefer, or use fennel seeds as an alternative.*

Makes 1 loaf

**Prep + cook time 1 hour, plus
proofing time**

1 cup lukewarm water

1¼ teaspoons active dry yeast

2 tablespoons black molasses

2 tablespoons milk powder

2 tablespoons sunflower oil, plus
extra for greasing

2 teaspoons caraway seeds

1 teaspoon salt

1¼ cups rye flour, plus extra for
dusting

2½ cups whole-wheat flour

¼ plain or orange-flavored 1000 mg
vitamin C tablet

1. Add the measured water, yeast, and molasses to the bowl of
a stand mixer with a dough hook and swirl the mix until
the yeast dissolves. Then add the milk powder, oil, caraway
seeds, and salt. Spoon in the flours and make a slight dip in
the center. Crush the vitamin C tablet using a spoon, then
add to the flour.

2. Knead on the lowest speed for about 5 minutes or until the
mixture has formed a smooth, stretchy dough.

3. Place the dough in a lightly greased bowl, cover with
plastic wrap, and leave until the dough has doubled in size,
about 1½ hours.

4. Tip the dough out onto a lightly floured surface and
knock back by pushing the air out. Put the dough into a
greased and lined 4-cup loaf pan, smooth side down. Cover
with a clean dish towel and leave somewhere warm for
about 30 minutes to let the bread rise.

5. Bake at 425°F for 40 minutes or until the loaf sounds
hollow when tapped underneath. Leave to cool in the
pan for 10 minutes and then turn out onto a wire rack
to cool completely.

*Ah, what else can I wish than eternal happiness, and that
we two, so long as we live, may have health, and strength,
and our necessary daily bread? For the third thing I know
not what to wish for.*

The Poor Man and the Rich Man

Mixed Seed Soda Bread

Buttermilk is the key to this bread, as it reacts with the baking soda to make the bread rise. If you don't have buttermilk, you can replace with it with a 50:50 mix of milk and plain yogurt, or add 1 tablespoon of lemon juice to milk and let it stand for 10 minutes to sour.

Makes 1 small loaf

Prep + cook time 1 hour

3 cups whole-wheat all-purpose flour, plus extra for dusting and sprinkling

½ cup sunflower seeds

2 tablespoons poppy seeds

1 teaspoon baking soda

1 teaspoon salt

1 teaspoon superfine sugar

1⅓ cups buttermilk

1. Lightly grease a cookie sheet. Mix the flour, sunflower and poppy seeds, baking soda, salt, and sugar together in a bowl.

2. Make a well in the center, add the buttermilk, and gradually work into the flour mixture to form a soft dough.

3. Turn the dough out onto a lightly floured surface and knead for 5 minutes. Shape into a flattish round. Transfer to the prepared cookie sheet. Using a sharp knife, cut a cross in the top of the bread and sprinkle a little extra flour over the surface.

4. Bake at 450°F for 15 minutes, then reduce the temperature to 400°F and bake for an additional 25–30 minutes until risen and the loaf sounds hollow when tapped underneath. Leave to cool on the cookie sheet for 10 minutes, then tranfer onto a wire rack to cool completely.

Classic Pretzels

These are delicious as they are, but for a sweet treat, you could go one better with chocolate pretzels. Melt ½ cup milk chocolate and drizzle random lines over the cooled pretzels with a spoon. Leave to harden, then repeat with ½ cup melted white chocolate.

Makes 40

Prep + cook time 40 minutes, plus proofing and setting

2 cups all-purpose flour, plus extra for dusting

1 teaspoon active dry yeast

2 teaspoons superfine sugar

pinch of salt

1 tablespoon melted butter, plus extra for greasing

½ cup warm water

For the glaze

2 teaspoons salt

½ teaspoon superfine sugar

2 tablespoons water

1. Mix the flour, yeast, sugar, and salt in a mixing bowl. Add the melted butter and gradually mix in the warm water until you have a smooth dough. Knead the dough for 5 minutes on a lightly floured surface until smooth and elastic.

2. Cut the dough into quarters, then cut each quarter into 10 smaller pieces. Shape each piece into a thin rope about 8 inches long. Bend the rope so that it forms a wide arc, then bring one of the ends around in a loop and secure about halfway along the rope. Do the same with the other end, looping it across the first secured end.

3. Transfer the pretzels to two greased cookie sheets. Cover loosely with lightly oiled plastic wrap and leave in a warm place for 30 minutes until well risen.

4. Bake at 400°F for 6–8 minutes until golden brown.

5. Meanwhile, make the glaze by adding all the ingredients to a small saucepan and heating gently until the salt and sugar have dissolved.

6. Brush the pretzels with the glaze as soon as they come out of the oven, then transfer to a wire rack to cool.

Butter and Milk

In peasant economies across the globe, the cow (or other dairy livestock such as the buffalo, goat, or yak) is the primary symbol of wealth and prosperity. A peasant without a cow (or a goat or a yak) is a very poor one indeed. No cow equals no milk, equals no butter and cheese, and no possibility of a calf and so no hope of a better future. In an agrarian, pre-industrial world, the lack of a cow can be, quite simply, a matter of life and death.

Unsurprisingly, then, folk and fairy tales—stories largely told by peasants, and about them, too—feature cows quite often.

One of the Grimms' own tales, "The Little Peasant," begins with a cow and a seeming act of foolishness. A peasant is so poor that he cannot afford to buy a cow. Instead, he asks a carpenter to make him a wooden calf, which, he hopes, will somehow magically transform into a real one. The wooden calf is stolen while in the care of the village cowherd, so the peasant takes him before a judge, who orders the appellant to give the plaintiff a real calf . . . and so this wildly surreal tale continues—until the peasant, becoming ever wiser and wilier, ends up the richest man in his village, with the tables turned and no doubt a whole herd of cows to his name.

The significance of owning a cow also crops up in other tales, such as "Lean Betty," in which Lean Betty says to her husband that, with four florins, she could buy a young cow. "It pleases me to think," her husband replies, "that if the cow should produce a calf, I could then refresh myself often with a draft of milk!"

We may not own a cow (or a goat or a yak) ourselves, but we should reverence them—and the milk they give us—all the same. The following recipes will show you how.

Chili Spice Butter

This versatile butter is perfect for perking up plain fish and poultry or topping barbecued meat, green and root vegetables, or new potatoes. It's also a useful freezer standby for stirring into pasta dishes, soups, and vegetable stews, or even a simple risotto.

Serves 4–6

Prep time 10 minutes, plus chilling

2 teaspoons cumin seeds

1 teaspoon coriander seeds

1 red chili, deseeded and finely chopped

2 scallions, trimmed and finely chopped

1 plump garlic clove, crushed

½ cup unsalted butter, softened

¼ teaspoon sea salt

2 tablespoons finely chopped parsley or cilantro

1. Put the cumin and coriander seeds into a small skillet and heat gently for about 1 minute until just beginning to color. Transfer to a mortar and grind until lightly crushed.

2. Tip into a bowl and add the chili, scallions, garlic, butter, salt, and parsley or cilantro.

3. Beat the mixture with a wooden spoon until evenly combined.

4. If you're not using the butter immediately, it can be shaped into a roll and chilled for up to two days, or frozen for several weeks. Turn the mixture onto a strip of waxed paper and bring the sides of the paper up over the butter, gently squeezing it into a sausage shape about 1¼ inches in diameter.

5. Chill or freeze the butter until you are ready to use it. If it is frozen, leave it at room temperature for 20–30 minutes before serving to get the best flavor.

Fresh Herb Butter

So easy to make, flavored butter is a great simple sauce. This herbed butter will melt irresistibly over grilled, baked, or pan-fried meat or fish. And try it over hot vegetables or swirled into bean or lentil soups.

Serves 4–6

Prep time 5 minutes, plus chilling

½ cup unsalted butter, softened

¼ teaspoon salt

2 tablespoons finely chopped parsley

2 tablespoons finely snipped chives

2 teaspoons lemon juice

black pepper

1. Put the butter into a small bowl with the salt, parsley, chives, lemon juice, and several grinds of black pepper. (Unsalted butter is best, but if you only have salted, leave out the additional salt.)

2. Beat the mixture with a wooden spoon until evenly combined.

3. If you're not using the butter immediately, it can be shaped into a roll and chilled for up to two days, or frozen for several weeks, a worthwhile way of using up a large quantity of fresh herbs. Turn the mixture onto a strip of waxed paper and bring the sides of the paper up over the butter, gently squeezing it into a sausage shape about 1¼ inches in diameter.

4. Chill or freeze the butter until you are ready to use it. If it is frozen, leave it at room temperature for 20–30 minutes before serving.

Brandy Butter

Strictly for the grown-ups, this boozy butter is traditionally served with Christmas pudding in the UK but is just as delicious decadently dolloped on top of an array of hot desserts: think apple pie, bread pudding, berry crumble, hot gingerbread, or peach cobbler.

Serves 6

Prep time 10−15 minutes

¾ cup unsalted butter, softened

¾ cup confectioners' sugar, sifted

thinly grated zest of ½ orange, plus a few thinly pared strips to garnish

2 tablespoons brandy

1. Put the butter in a bowl and, using an electric or handheld rotary whisk, beat until light and fluffy. Gradually beat in the confectioners' sugar, then beat in the orange zest and the brandy.

2. Turn the brandy butter into a serving bowl and chill in the refrigerator until quite firm. Serve garnished with thinly pared strips of orange rind.

Cinnamon Butter

Lavish this sweet delight onto hot toast, fruity scones, waffles, Sunday morning pancakes, warm English muffins, homemade bread, and more. Super easy and super fast, this cinnamon butter will definitely take breakfast up a notch.

Serves 8

Prep time 5 minutes

½ cup unsalted butter, softened

1 teaspoon ground cinnamon

½ teaspoon vanilla extract (optional)

2–3 tablespoons confectioners' sugar, sifted

1. In a bowl, beat the butter, cinnamon, and vanilla extract, if using. Add the confectioners' sugar a little at a time, until the butter is the sweetness you like. Mix together until completely smooth.

2. Store in an airtight container in the refrigerator and serve at room temperature for easy spreading.

Almond Milk

For a great dairy-free refresher on a hot day, try this Moroccan-inspired recipe. Laced with fragrant orange blossom water, it's hard to resist. To serve in the traditional way, you could sprinkle a little ground cinnamon on top.

Serves 4

Prep + cook time 30 minutes

⅔ cup blanched almonds

2½ cups water

½ cup granulated sugar

1 tablespoon orange blossom water

ice cubes, to serve (optional)

1. Place the almonds in a food processor and blend to a smooth paste, adding a splash of water to loosen.

2. Place the measured water and sugar in a heavy-based saucepan and bring to a boil, stirring continuously until the sugar has dissolved. Stir in the almond paste and simmer for 5 minutes. Stir in the orange blossom water and turn off the heat.

3. Leave to cool in the pan to let the flavors mingle, then pass through a cheesecloth into a jug and squeeze tightly to extract all the milky liquid from the almonds.

4. Pour into four glasses, add some ice cubes to each, and serve immediately. Alternatively, chill in the refrigerator before serving.

Chilled Vanilla Milk

Both kids and adults will love this ice-cold vanilla milk—just add a straw and enjoy! You could use maple syrup, honey, or agave syrup to sweeten instead of the sugar, if you prefer. And, to warm cold hands on a chilly day, pour into mugs and microwave until hot.

Serves 4

Prep + cook time 20 minutes

2½ cups milk

2 vanilla pods

superfine sugar, to taste

ice cubes, to serve (optional)

1. Add the milk and vanilla pods to a heavy-based saucepan over gentle heat and bring to just below boiling point. Turn off the heat, stir in sugar to taste, and leave to cool.

2. Remove the vanilla pods, slit open lengthwise, and scrape out the seeds. Strain the milk into a jug, stir in the seeds, and pour into four glasses over ice cubes. Alternatively, chill in the refrigerator before serving.

The bird put the key into the girl's hand and said, "Do you see yon great tree? Within it is a cupboard, which is opened with this key, and there you will find food enough, so that you need not suffer hunger any longer." The girl went to the tree and, unlocking it, found pure milk in a jug, and white bread fit to break into it; and of these she made a good meal.

The Old Woman in the Wood

Don't Tell the Children

Despite the title of the collection, *Children's and Household Tales*, the eighty-six stories published by the Brothers Grimm in the first (1812) edition were by no means written with children in mind. The collection of the *Tales* was above all an academic endeavor: the brothers worked as court librarians in Kassel, the stories were accompanied by an extensive scholarly commentary, and the subject matter was often dark and grotesque. There was little pretense about their having "adult" themes—sex and violence, oppression and poverty—and many contemporary critics expressed their horror that these strange, barbarous tales could ever be considered suitable as children's bedtime reading. Jacob and Wilhelm Grimm had worked on the project from at least 1806, and their intention had always been to capture the genuine, folkloric voice of the Volk, the common people—the oral tales passed down through the generations from medieval times and beyond.

In this respect, the project was part of a wider revival in interest in a deep-seated, "national" Germanic, or Teutonic, culture at a time when "Germany" as a single unified state did not yet exist. This in turn was part of the wider Romantic movement across Europe that sought to throw off the shackles of classical, elitist, pan-continental culture—led by France—and rediscover the local and the national, the primitive and the pure. Perhaps the clearest expression of the Romantic spirit, in the eyes of many, was the works of Ossian, the supposedly ancient Gaelic poet whose epic fragments the modern poet James Macpherson (1736–96) claimed to have "discovered" and "translated," but which in reality were fabrications of often dubious quality. Macpherson's claims were quickly contested, but this did not stop them from becoming influential across Europe, especially in Germany, as a genuine, unadulterated expression of a Volk.

The *Tales* likewise proved a fraught and compromised endeavor, as the Grimms themselves quickly realized. While the brothers liked to claim that the tales were gathered from oral sources, told to them by peasants and other working people, many of their storytellers were in fact literate, middle class, and even aristocratic, among them Wilhelm's future wife, Dorothea Wild; the artist Philipp Otto Runge; and the aristocratic scientist and lawyer August von Haxthausen. The *Tales* were

far from being purely Germanic, too—many, including such well-known tales as "Briar-Rose," were French in origin, passed on by tellers with Huguenot ancestry. The very idea of a "pure" fairy tale was an impossible dream. As folklorists have subsequently ascertained, stories permeate freely across cultures, languages, and traditions, growing, adapting, hybridizing, and localizing as they go.

The Grimms, especially Wilhelm, tried to address such issues through later editions, expunging tales that had clear French or literary antecedents and editing the tales so that they seemed more "German" and folkish. This extended as far as the vocabulary: out went French-derived words like *Prinzessin* ("princess") and *Fee* ("fay" or "fairy") and in came purely German ones like *Königstochter* ("king's daughter") and *Zauberin* ("sorceress"). The seventh edition, published in 1857, was thus a very different kettle of fish from its 1812 forebear. Now there were 210 stories, the plots had been "clarified," and literary details and color added. The violence had been toned down, Christian values and didactic messages emphasized, and sex had been banished altogether: no longer did Rapunzel have to worry about why her gown was beginning to fit so snugly about her belly! The *Tales* had become both more Teutonic and child-friendly, reflected in the gorgeously illustrated editions that now began to appear. Translated versions, especially those of Victorian Britain, expurgated and prettified the texts still further.

Perhaps the Grimms need not have worried so much about the suitability of the *Tales* for children: in his lecture-essay "On Fairy-Stories" (1947), the philologist and writer J. R. R. Tolkien, who had read the *Tales* in translation as a child and deeply admired the brothers' academic work, wrote that children should not be protected from the facts of life, especially in stories. Grimm tales like "The Juniper Tree" (see pages 128 and 138), for all their violence and horror, had a powerful, mythic effect on the reader, who forgot the gruesomeness but remembered the haunting power: "Without the [human] stew and the bones—which children are now too often spared in mollified versions of Grimm—that vision would largely have been lost." These are tales we should tell our children.

Crumbs & Nibbles

We've had our hearty breakfast and, with a full stomach, we've set off bravely on our adventure. Our home is soon far behind us, we've walked a long way along the road, and have seen all sorts of wonders and met all sorts of people along the way. Now, though, our feet are a little sore and we feel a bit peckish. And wouldn't it be nice if we could lie down for a while on a soft bed? The problem is, we suddenly notice, we've come to a deep, dark forest and—wouldn't you know?—we've forgotten to bring our stick and bindle in which we'd so carefully packed a hunk of bread, an apple, and some cheese. "Oh no!" we wail.

Just then we spot smoke curling out of a chimney. It's a tiny thatched cottage almost hidden among the trees. A delicious fragrance wafts toward us—something wonderful must be cooking up on the stove . . . Perhaps if we knock at the door and politely ask for a bite to eat, the owner will ask us in to join them at their table. It will be just something light until we get home again . . .

Knock, knock . . .

Rapunzel's Mother's Salad

The luxuriantly tressed heroine of the Grimms' tale "Rapunzel" gets her name from an edible plant. The not-so-well-known beginning of the story tells how a childless woman hankers after the *rapunzel* growing in her neighbor's high-walled garden, this neighbor happening to be a sorceress. So great is the woman's desire to eat the plant, her husband climbs over the wall and steals some. The wife eats it in a fresh green salad, but this only seems to make her want more, so her husband dutifully repeats the process the following night, but this time he is caught red-handed by the sorceress. Instead of punishing him, however, she promises to allow his wife to eat as much *rapunzel* as she likes, as long as the couple gives her their first-born child. When the woman gives birth to a daughter not so long after, the sorceress immediately takes the child to bring up as her own, calling her Rapunzel after the plant.

What on earth is *rapunzel*, we may wonder, and why would anyone develop such a taste for it? The German use the term for several edible plants—is it a rampion, as many English translations give, with its spinachlike leaves and radishlike roots, or is it lamb's lettuce? No one seems to know for sure. Either of these would be suitable enough for the mother's salad, but tasty as these no doubt are, they would surely not be worth dying over.

The mystery begins to be solved when we return to the earlier, non-German versions of the tale, where the plant the mother craves is not rampion but parsley, and her daughter's name is accordingly Persinette (in French) or Petrosinella (in Italian), both meaning "little parsley." Parsley was traditionally associated with fertility and sexual desire: in English folklore, the saying goes, "to sow parsley is to sow children," and babies were said to be found in parsley beds. In these versions the meaning of the woman's obsession becomes much clearer—she wants sex and she wants a child.

We cannot quite promise our vegetable salad here will have such an aphrodisiac effect, but it will certainly leave you hankering for more!

When spring arrives we crave lighter, brighter dishes after winter's hearty soups and stews. And nothing says spring quite like a fragrant, herby tabbouleh. Bejeweled with vibrant carrots and beets and topped with tangy feta, this is a colorful dish to lift the spirits and welcome in the sunshine of spring.

Serves 4

Prep + cook time 25 minutes

1 cup bulgur wheat

1 garlic clove, crushed

pinch of ground cinnamon

pinch of ground allspice

2 tablespoons pomegranate molasses

5 tablespoons extra-virgin olive oil

1 carrot, peeled and grated

1 cup ready-cooked beets, cubed

2 scallions, sliced

½ green chili, chopped

large handful of mint, chopped

large handful of parsley, chopped

1 cup feta cheese, crumbled

salt and pepper

1. Put the bulgur wheat in a bowl, pour over enough boiling water to cover the wheat by 2 inches, and leave to soak for 20 minutes. Alternatively, prepare the bulgur wheat according to the package instructions, then drain thoroughly.

2. Mix together the garlic, spices, pomegranate molasses, and olive oil. Toss together with the bulgur wheat, carrot, beets, scallions, chili, mint, and parsley and season to taste. Sprinkle with the feta to serve.

Each day her craving grew . . . and she grew pale and thin. Her husband was alarmed, and asked, "What is the matter, dear wife?" "Oh," she answered, "If I don't get any of the rapunzels from the garden behind our house, I will die."

Rapunzel

The Robber Bride's
Lentil and Sardine Salad

The Grimms' *Tales* often delight in the goriest of details that, like scenes of a modern horror movie, linger in the mind. Such occurs in "The Robber-Bridegroom," where the heroine, visiting her betrothed in his forest abode, discovers that he is the leader of a band of cannibal robbers. En route, she sets a trail of peas and lentils so that she can reach home easily after her visit.

On reaching the house, an old woman tells her that her husband-to-be is not the respectable man he pretends to be and warns her that, on their return, he and his band will kill and eat her. Just in time, the girl hides behind a barrel as the band of robbers turns up with a captive girl, whom they proceed to kill and dismember. During this horrific crime, one of the victim's fingers is chopped off with such force that it flies through the air and lands in the hidden girl's lap. On it is a gold ring.

The old woman gives the robbers a sleeping potion, and she and the girl make their escape, following the trail of peas and lentils that have in the meantime sprouted. On her wedding day, the girl's betrothed turns up as handsome and respectable as ever. The girl recounts the strange "dream" she has had, about a visit to her groom's forest den. Finally, she reaches the moment where the bloody finger lands in her lap . . . and produces the ring itself. The robber is arrested and executed for his crimes.

Here we have a recipe featuring not lady's fingers (okra)—you'll be relieved to know—but the lentils that led the poor bride-to-be home.

Fiber-rich lentils make up the bulk of this delicious, quick-to-prepare salad. A hint of red onion and refreshing mint bring together the flavors.

Serves 4

Prep + cook time 20 minutes

¾ cup frozen peas

2 x 3¾-oz. cans boneless, skinless
   sardines in tomato sauce

14½-oz. can green lentils, rinsed
   and drained

2 inches cucumber, diced

1 small red onion, finely chopped

small bunch of mint, chopped

grated zest and juice of 1 lemon

1 head of romaine lettuce

black pepper

1. Cook the peas in a saucepan of boiling water for 3 minutes. Alternatively, cook them in the microwave for 1½ minutes on full power.

2. Flake the sardines into chunks and put them in a large salad bowl with their sauce. Add the lentils, peas, cucumber, onion, mint, lemon zest and juice, and a little pepper and toss together.

3. Separate the lettuce into leaves and arrange them on serving plates. Spoon the sardine salad on top and serve.

"Forest Hut" Succotash

There is some toe-curling violence inflicted on animals in the Grimms' *Tales*—throats slit, eyes gouged, limbs sliced—so it is a relief to come across tales in which humans show loving kindness and compassion for the beasties. In "The White Snake," for example, the hero rescues a whole series of animals from mortal danger, and in "The Summer and Winter Garden"—a version of "Beauty and the Beast"—the heroine's kindness toward the Beast might be read as her expanding compassion for the "others" of the world, including its nonhuman animals.

Perhaps the most explicit tale of animal friendship occurs in "The Hut in the Forest," where, one by one, three sisters turn up at a cottage deep in the forest inhabited by an old man and his animal companions—a hen, a rooster, and a brindled cow. The first two sisters cook dinner only for the man and themselves, and are punished by being thrown into the cellar. The third, however, not only makes a human meal but thoughtfully gives barley to the birds and hay to the cow, and is rewarded by the old man turning into a handsome prince (whatever other reward could there be?).

In some versions of this tale the sisters lay trails of seeds, corn, and beans to help them find their way back out of the forest. So what, we may wonder, did the youngest sister cook for the old man's dinner? Here is our idea—a succotash—the Native American corn and bean dish that has become a classic of New England cuisine.

Derived from the Narragansett Native American word sohquttahhash, *meaning "broken corn kernels," succotash is a uniquely American dish that has many variations, but always contains corn kernels and some kind of bean, usually fava beans.*

Serves 4

Prep + cook time 20 minutes

4 corncobs

1 tablespoon olive oil

2 garlic cloves, crushed

1 green bell pepper, cored, deseeded, and diced

1 cup frozen fava beans

1 cup cherry tomatoes, halved

handful of basil leaves, torn

salt and black pepper

1. Use a knife to cut down the length of the corn to remove the kernels. Heat the oil in a large lidded pan. Cook the kernels, garlic, and green pepper over medium heat for 5 minutes, stirring all the time.

2. Add the frozen beans to the pan, cover, and cook, stirring every so often, for an additional 5 minutes or until the beans are cooked through. Turn off the heat and add the cherry tomatoes and basil. Season to taste and serve.

Cheese

Choosing a husband or a wife is an important theme in folk tales, reflecting of course the crucial importance of this decision in preindustrial society. A marriage could make all the difference between a happy, prosperous life and an unhappy, impoverished one; while romance was often certainly in the mix, economics was at the forefront of marital considerations. Folk tales, while often masquerading as romance—the prince falls in love and marries a poor miller's daughter—always have a rather more hardheaded side, too: the prince, being wealthy, can marry for love; it's his prerogative. The rest of us have to weigh up matters more cannily.

Though cheese makes an appearance in the *Tales* several times (such as in "The Valiant Little Tailor," "The Little Farmer," "Catherine and Frederick," and "Hans in Luck," the folkloric hardheadedness of the above is nowhere more apparent than in the Grimms' tale of "Choosing a Bride," taken from a Swiss source, in which a woman's treatment of a piece of cheese is seen to illustrate her worth as a marriage partner:

> *There was a young herdsman who wanted very much to marry, and was acquainted with three sisters. Each one was just as beautiful as the other, so it was difficult for him to make a choice, and he could not decide to give the preference to any one of them. Then he asked his mother for advice, and she said, "Invite all three, and set some cheese before them, and watch how they cut off a slice."*

> *The youth did so. The first one ate the cheese with the rind on. The second one hastily cut the rind off the cheese, but she cut it so quickly that she left much good cheese with it, and threw that away also. The third peeled the rind off carefully, and cut neither too much nor too little. The shepherd told all this to his mother, who said, "Take the third for your wife."*

Cheese was an important resource in an Alpine community, so what better guide for choosing a wife could the young herdsman adopt, especially when otherwise the women on offer seem so interchangeable? The moral of this tale? Use your cheese wisely when making the following recipes— you never know who may be watching . . . and judging!

Soft Cheese Dip

Every party needs a dip, and this super-easy one is a great choice. Serve it with potato chips, pretzels, crackers, or—for a healthier spin—crunchy veggie crudités, such as strips of pepper, baby carrots, broccoli florets, and cherry tomatoes.

Serves 4

Prep time 5 minutes

1 cup soft cheese

5 tablespoons milk

2 tablespoons chopped chives

1 tablespoon whole-grain mustard

black pepper

1. Place the soft cheese in a bowl with the milk and chives. Season generously with pepper, add the mustard, and mash well. Place in a small bowl and serve.

Potted Cheese

Potted cheese is a wonderful way to use up all those scraps of cheese from a cheeseboard, turning leftovers into something to wow dinner guests. Serve it as you would pâté, with hot toast, crackers, or crusty bread for a dinner party starter or snack.

Serves 8—10

Prep time 15 minutes

4½–5 cups hard cheese such as cheddar, grated

1 teaspoon mustard powder

½ teaspoon powdered mace

¼ teaspoon cayenne pepper

1½ cups butter

⅔ cup sweet sherry or white wine

¼ cup butter, melted

1. Place the grated cheese, mustard powder, mace, cayenne pepper, and butter in a food processor or blender and blitz to a smooth paste.

2. Add the sherry or wine gradually, blending each time until it is quite absorbed before adding more.

3. When the cheese mixture is creamy and smooth, put it into one large pot or several individual ramekins, pressing it down firmly to avoid air bubbles.

4. Pour the melted butter gently over the top. Leave undisturbed until it has set. Refrigerate until needed and take out of the refrigerator about 10 minutes before serving.

Beery Cheese Fondue

How did this retro favorite ever go out of fashion? It's such an easy and fun way to feed friends and family. Be sure to supply a variety of crunchy dippers to cut through the rich cheese, and stir the fondue as you dip to keep it from sticking to the bottom.

Serves 4

Prep + cook time 30 minutes

1 garlic clove

1 tablespoon cornstarch

¾ cup blonde beer or lager

1¾ cups Gruyère cheese, rind removed and grated

1½ cups Emmental cheese, rind removed and grated

grated nutmeg

salt and black pepper

To serve

½ loaf French bread, cubed

2 celery stalks, cut into short lengths

8 small pickled onions, drained and halved

1 bunch of radishes, tops trimmed

1 red bell pepper, cored, deseeded, and cubed

2 endives, leaves separated

1. Rub the inside of a fondue pot with the garlic clove.

2. Put the cornstarch in a small bowl and mix with a little of the beer to make a smooth paste, then add to the pot with the remaining beer. Add both the cheeses, a little nutmeg, and some salt and pepper.

3. Cook over moderate heat on the stovetop, gently stirring, for 10–15 minutes until creamy and smooth; don't overcook the fondue or it will get stringy.

4. Serve at once with the dippers arranged on a serving plate, with long fondue or ordinary forks for dunking the dippers into the fondue.

The husband said he had no objection, but bade her bring him quickly something to eat. The wife said, "I have nothing but bread and cheese," and her husband told her with that he should be contented, and asked the farmer to come and share his meal.

The Little Farmer

Baked Brie with Maple Syrup

You'll keep coming back to this indulgent and delicious recipe. Creamy, oozy, gooey melted cheese, topped with sweet and sticky maple syrup and crunchy pecans—what's not to love?

Serves 4

Prep + cook time 20 minutes

10 oz. whole baby Brie or
   Camembert

¼ cup pecans

3 tablespoons maple syrup

3 tablespoons soft dark brown sugar

thyme sprigs

crusty bread, to serve

1. Remove any plastic packaging from the cheese and return it to its wooden box. Place on a cookie sheet and bake at 400°F for 15 minutes.

2. Meanwhile, toast the pecans in a small skillet for 3–5 minutes until lightly browned, then set aside. Put the maple syrup and sugar in a small saucepan and bring to a boil. Cook for 1 minute until foamy.

3. Take the cheese from the oven and cut a small cross in the center. Drizzle over the maple syrup, sprinkle with the pecans and thyme, and serve with plenty of crusty bread.

"Where are the butter and cheese?" cried her husband. "Oh, Fred, dear," she replied, "with the butter I have smeared the ruts, and the cheeses will soon come, but one ran away, and I sent the others after it to call it back!"

"It was silly of you to do so," said Fred, "to grease the roads with butter, and to roll cheeses down the hill!"

"If you had but told me so," said Catherine, vexatiously.

Catherine and Frederick

Caramelized Onion and Cheese Toasts

That perennial favorite, the grilled cheese sandwich, gets a lift here with the addition of sweet onion chutney. Eat it as soon as you comfortably can to get the most of the gooey melted cheese filling. To ring the changes, swap the chutney for whole-grain mustard or cranberry sauce.

Serves 2

Prep + cook time 15 minutes

4 slices of sourdough bread

2 tablespoons caramelized onion chutney

2¼ cups Gruyère cheese, grated

1 large egg

2 tablespoons milk

1 tablespoon sunflower oil

salt and black pepper

1. Spread two slices of the bread with the chutney, then divide the cheese equally between them. Top with the remaining slices of bread to make two sandwiches.

2. Beat the egg and milk together in a shallow bowl and season to taste. Heat the oil in a large nonstick skillet.

3. Place the sandwiches in the egg mixture. Leave for 1 minute, then turn over and leave for an additional minute.

4. Cook the sandwiches in the skillet for 3 minutes on each side until golden brown and the cheese has melted. Serve immediately.

Cheesy Chips

These tasty chips are great to serve with pre-dinner drinks, or to float on top of soup when you want to impress. You can vary the flavor by adding a little black or cayenne pepper or dried basil if you like.

Serves 6

Prep + cook time 15 minutes

1½ cups mature cheddar, Gruyère, or Parmesan, finely grated

1. Line several cookie sheets with nonstick baking paper. Place two mounds of cheese on each sheet, about 3½ inches in diameter and at least 4 inches apart as the cheese will spread and form cookie shapes.

2. Bake at 425°F for 10 minutes, until the cheese bubbles and begins to turn a very pale cream color. Do not overcook or the cheese will taste bitter.

3. Allow the chips to cool slightly, then transfer them to a wire rack using a spatula, and let them cool completely. Store in an airtight container.

Ash Cakes

"Cinderella," or "Aschenputtel" (the German name for Cinderella), is the archetypal rags-to-riches story: the tale of a young, impoverished woman who, by dint of her beauty, her goodness, and perhaps a little bit of magic, finally gets her just deserts, marries a rich man (a prince, preferably), and lives happily ever after.

Ashes are a central motif in the tale—giving the heroine not only her name but the outward sign of her debasement. She sleeps in ashes, her face is smudged with soot, and her clothes are thick with coal dust. Perhaps all she would have had to eat is something similar to these ash cakes, made from flour and water . . . The ashes, however, also hint at Cinderella's potential for renewal and resurgence. The mythical bird, the phoenix, is repeatedly reborn out of the ashes of its old self—an image that echoes down through the ages. Aschenputtel's story itself has proved endlessly recyclable, endlessly renewable—so that, whatever one may think of its gendered stereotyping, it will likely live on, in new and surprising variants, for ages to come.

The smoky notes that the coals impart in this recipe give them a lovely rustic flavor. If cooking on coals doesn't appeal, you can also cook them on a lightly oiled barbecue grill for 15–20 minutes, flipping halfway. Serve hot, smeared with butter and honey, or, for a savory version, with the herb butter on page 49.

Makes 6–8

Prep + cook time 45 minutes plus proofing time

8 cups all-purpose flour, plus extra for dusting

pinch of salt

1 tablespoon granulated sugar

2 teaspoons active dry yeast

2 tablespoons vegetable oil, plus extra for greasing

approximately 3 cups lukewarm water

1. Sift the flour and salt together into a large bowl. Add the sugar and yeast. Add the oil and enough lukewarm water to mix to a soft, sticky dough. Add more water if necessary.

2. Turn the dough out onto a lightly floured surface and knead for 5 minutes, or until it is smooth and elastic. Place the dough in a large, lightly oiled bowl, cover with a clean dish towel, and leave to rise in a warm place for about 30 minutes or until doubled in size.

3. Knock the dough down on a lightly floured surface and knead until smooth. Divide into six to eight pieces and roll into smooth balls. Cover again with the dish towel and leave to rise in a warm place for about 15 minutes or until the balls of dough are well risen.

4. Place the balls in the warm ashes of the fire, among the coals. Cook for about 20 minutes or until they sound hollow on the bottom when tapped with your knuckles. Use a pastry brush to brush off any excess ashes before serving.

At night, when she was tired, she had no bed to lie on, but was forced to sit in the ashes on the hearth; and because she looked dirty through this, they named her Cinderella.

Cinderella

There was a little garden belonging to the charmed house, in which stood twelve lilies . . . and the sister, thinking to give her twelve brothers a pleasure, broke off the twelve flowers, intending to give each of them one.

The Twelve Brothers

Flower Garden Sandwiches

The garden has long been a recurring motif of folklore and myth—a locus of wonders and transformations. From the Garden of Eden in the book of Genesis to *The Secret Garden* (1912) by Frances Hodgson Burnett, the garden, with its trees and flowers, streams and ponds, has been the place in which the hero and heroine make new discoveries about the world and themselves and, under its influence, undergo a profound metamorphosis—social, spiritual, and even physical, perhaps from a prince to a toad and back again! It's no coincidence that folk tales quite often begin in gardens—symbolic sites of regeneration and alchemy.

Significant "garden" episodes occur in many of the Grimms' tales—the king's walled orchard in "The Girl with No Hands," the sorceress's kitchen garden in "Rapunzel," the cottage garden with two rose trees, one white, one red, at the beginning of "Snow-White and Rose-Red" . . . The brothers themselves had a deep love of gardens, especially of the Baroque garden of Wilhelmshöhe, in their homeland of North Hesse, which itself might be the setting of a fairy tale.

Make these pretty sandwiches and you will set the scene for any fairy-tale picnic.

Get creative with these cute flower-shaped sandwiches. You can vary the filling—try thinly sliced turkey, ham, cucumber, or cheese. And you don't have to stick to one particular flower shape—be as creative as you like.

Serves 8

Prep time 20 minutes

2 teaspoons basil pesto

1 cup soft cheese

8 slices of white bread

8 slices of whole-wheat bread

2 cherry tomatoes, halved

2 green grapes, halved

1 pack mustard and cress

1 large carrot, peeled and sliced

1. Mix together the pesto and soft cheese in a bowl, then spread over the white bread. Cover with the whole-wheat bread and press together firmly. Using a medium-size cutter, cut out as many flower shapes as you can.

2. Cut a small circle out of the center of each sandwich using an apple corer and stick either a cherry tomato half or a grape half in the middle.

3. Arrange on a plate or board on a bed of mustard and cress. Cut small flower shapes from the carrot slices using a small cutter and sprinkle over the "grass."

Soup

Sometimes all we could wish for is a bowl of soup—comforting, hearty, nourishing. Cooked in just one pot, soup exemplifies the notion of food as sharing, as a symbol of community. Served in a simple bowl, it symbolizes the idea of food as a gift—the bowl standing in for the cupped hands. The symbolism of soup is captured in the well-known European folk tale "Stone Soup," or "Axe Soup," in which hungry travelers trick at first unwelcoming villagers into making small contributions to a cooking pot that, over the cooking time, builds up into a delicious soup that everyone can share. Something of this symbolism of soup may also be found in the Grimms' fairy tale "Sweet Oatmeal"—sometimes, indeed, translated as "Sweet Soup"—in which a family acquires a cooking pot that creates oatmeal/soup for everyone, as much as they can eat . . . though, here, with ultimately disastrous consequences.

Soup also appears prominently in the Brothers Grimm tale "Cat-skin." Here the Cinderella-like heroine—a princess in disguise who goes by the name of "Cat-skin" and who works as an ash-besmirched scullery maid—woos the king by making him the best soup he has ever tasted. She makes the soup several times, concealing treasures at the bottom of a bowl—a ring, a necklace, and a brooch—and it is by the means of the ring that her true identity is at last revealed. The tale leaves us in some doubt as to whether it is the delicious soup or the princess's radiant beauty that has captured the king's heart.

> *Cat-skin heated the king's soup, and toasted a slice of bread first, as nicely as ever she could; and when it was ready, she went and looked in the cabin for her little golden ring, and put it into the dish in which the soup was. When the dance was over, the king ordered his soup to be brought in; and it pleased him so well, that he thought he had never tasted any so good before.*

Broccoli and Almond Soup

Tasty, filling, and full of good-for-you fiber, protein, vitamins, and minerals, this soup can be on the table in 30 minutes—ideal for those winter nights when you get home tired and hungry. Delicious with a thick slice of the Rye and Caraway Bread on page 44.

Serves 6

Prep + cook time 30 minutes

2 tablespoons butter

1 onion, roughly chopped

8 cups broccoli, cut into florets, stems sliced

½ cup ground almonds

3⅔ cups vegetable or chicken stock (see page 38)

1¼ cups milk

salt and black pepper

To garnish

1 tablespoon butter

6 tablespoons plain yogurt

3 tablespoons slivered almonds

1. Heat the butter in a saucepan, add the onion, and fry gently for 5 minutes until just beginning to soften. Stir in the broccoli until coated in the butter, then add the ground almonds, stock, and a little salt and pepper.

2. Bring to a boil, then cover and simmer for 10 minutes until the broccoli is just tender and still bright green. Leave to cool slightly, then puree in batches in a blender or food processor until finely speckled with green.

3. Pour the puree back into the saucepan and stir in the milk. Reheat, then taste and adjust the seasoning if needed. Heat the 1 tablespoon butter in a skillet, add the almonds, and fry for a few minutes, stirring until golden. Ladle the soup into bowls, drizzle a spoonful of yogurt over each bowl, then sprinkle with the slivered almonds.

Chicken and Corn Chowder

When you need a meal in minutes, sink your spoon into this quick and easy chowder. It's a great way to use up scraps of leftover roast chicken. To ring the changes, try it with canned crabmeat instead of the chicken and, if you want to squeeze in more of your five a day, you could add some frozen peas.

Serves 4

Prep + cook time 20 minutes

11-oz. can creamed corn

1¾ cups milk

1¼ cups cooked chicken, torn into pieces

1 cup frozen corn kernels

2 scallions, chopped

2 teaspoons cornstarch

salt and black pepper

1. Place the creamed corn in a saucepan with the milk and heat, stirring.

2. Add the chicken, corn kernels, and scallions and season with salt and pepper. Simmer for 5 minutes, stirring occasionally.

3. Blend the cornstarch with 1 tablespoon water, pour into the soup, and stir to thicken. Ladle into bowls and serve.

Beef and Barley Broth

Loaded with chunks of tender meat, plump barley, and plenty of veggies, this is pure comfort in a bowl. Easy to make—just a little chopping and stirring—it improves with keeping and freezes well so is a great make-ahead meal to prep over the weekend.

Serves 6

Prep + cook time 2 hours 10 minutes

2 tablespoons butter

2¾ cups boneless braising beef, trimmed of fat and cut into small cubes

1 large onion, finely chopped

1⅔ cups rutabaga, diced

1 cup diced carrots

½ cup pearl barley

8 cups beef stock

2 teaspoons mustard powder (optional)

salt and black pepper

chopped parsley, to garnish

1. Melt the butter in a large saucepan, add the beef and onion, and fry for 5 minutes, stirring, until the beef is browned and the onion is just beginning to color.

2. Stir in the diced vegetables, pearl barley, stock, and mustard powder, if using. Season with salt and pepper and bring to a boil. Reduce the heat, cover, and simmer for 1¾ hours until the meat and vegetables are very tender, stirring occasionally. Taste and adjust the seasoning if needed.

3. Ladle the soup into bowls and sprinkle with a little chopped parsley.

Chestnut Soup with Truffle Oil

Silky smooth with the earthy taste of chestnuts and laced with brandy and truffle oil, this is a special soup worthy of a special occasion. It takes a bit of time to prep but the result is worth it. Serve it as a light meal or a starter for a dinner party.

Serves 6

Prep + cook time 1½ hours

4⅔ cups fresh chestnuts

½ cup butter

1 onion, finely chopped

10 smoked bacon slices

1⅓ cups potatoes, diced

4 tablespoons brandy, plus a little extra to serve (optional)

3¾ cups pheasant or beef stock

fresh thyme sprig

large pinch of ground cinnamon

large pinch of grated nutmeg

salt and black pepper

truffle oil, to garnish

1. Make a cross cut in the top of each chestnut, then add to a saucepan of boiling water and poach for 15 minutes. Drain into a colander, rinse with cold water so that they are cool enough to handle, then remove the skins with a small sharp knife and chop roughly.

2. Heat the butter in a saucepan, add the onion, and fry gently for 5 minutes until just beginning to turn golden around the edges. Dice four slices of the bacon and add to the pan along with the potatoes and chestnuts. Fry gently for 5 minutes, stirring occasionally.

3. Add the brandy and, when bubbling, flame with a long taper and quickly stand back. As soon as the flames have subsided, pour in the stock. Add the thyme, spices, and seasoning and bring to a boil, cover, and simmer for 45 minutes.

4. Discard the thyme sprig and puree half the soup in a blender or food processor until smooth. Return to the soup in the pan and reheat. Taste and adjust the seasoning if needed. Wrap each remaining slice of bacon around a skewer and grill until crisp. Ladle the soup into cups and top with the bacon skewers. Drizzle with the truffle oil and a little extra brandy if desired.

. . . a third fete was given by the king, at which everything went as before. The cook said to Allerleirauh when she asked leave to go, "You are certainly a witch, and always put something in the soup which makes it taste better than mine. Still, since you beg so hard, you shall go at the usual time."

Allerleirauh

Basque Fish Soup

Enjoy the flavors of Spain in this delicious soup that simmers heart-healthy mackerel in a heavenly wine, tomato, and paprika broth. Serve with lemon wedges for squeezing over and plenty of crusty bread for mopping up every last drop.

Serves 6

Prep + cook time 1 hour

2 tablespoons olive oil

1 onion, finely chopped

½ green bell pepper, cored, deseeded, and diced

½ red bell pepper, cored, deseeded, and diced

1 zucchini, diced

2 garlic cloves, finely chopped

3 cups potatoes, cut into chunks

½ teaspoon smoked paprika

⅔ cup red wine

4 cups fish stock

14-oz. can chopped tomatoes

1 tablespoon tomato paste

2 whole mackerel, gutted and rinsed with cold water inside and out

cayenne pepper

salt

lemon wedges, to serve

1. Heat the oil in a large saucepan, add the onion, and fry gently for 5 minutes until softened. Add the peppers, zucchini, garlic, and potatoes and fry for 5 minutes, stirring. Mix in the paprika and cook for 1 minute.

2. Pour in the wine, stock, tomatoes, tomato paste, and salt and cayenne pepper to taste. Bring to a boil, stirring, then add the whole mackerel. Reduce the heat, cover, and simmer gently for 20 minutes until the fish flakes easily when pressed with a knife.

3. Lift the fish out with a slotted spoon and put on a plate. Simmer the soup, uncovered, for an additional 15 minutes. Peel the skin off the fish, then lift the fish away from the backbone. Flake into pieces, checking carefully for any remaining bones.

4. Return the mackerel flakes to the soup and reheat. Ladle into shallow bowls and serve with lemon wedges.

Celery Root and Apple Soup

Low in carbs, high in nutrients, celery root, with its nutty, celery flavor and velvety texture, creates a beautifully smooth and warming soup. Add the sweetness of apples and you have a tasty and comforting midweek meal or elegant first course.

Serves 6

Prep + cook time 40 minutes

2 tablespoons butter

1 celery root, about 6 cups, peeled and coarsely grated

3 dessert apples, peeled, cored, and chopped

5 cups vegetable or chicken stock (see page 38)

pinch of cayenne pepper, or more to taste

salt

To garnish

2–3 tablespoons finely diced dessert apple

paprika

1. Melt the butter in a large saucepan and cook the celery root and apples over medium heat for 5 minutes or until they have begun to soften.

2. Add the stock and cayenne pepper and bring to a boil. Reduce the heat, cover the pan, and simmer for 15–20 minutes or until the celery root and apples are very soft.

3. Puree the mixture in a blender or food processor until it is very smooth, transferring each batch to a clean saucepan. Alternatively, rub through a fine strainer. Reheat gently. Season to taste and serve in individual bowls, garnished with the finely diced apple and a dusting of paprika.

Pea and Lentil Soup with Crispy Cured Ham

When it's cold outside, curled up in front of the fire with a bowl of thick, hearty soup is the place to be. Quick to prepare, using convenient canned lentils and garbanzo beans, this is sure to become a go-to recipe for the winter months.

Serves 4

Prep + cook time 15 minutes

¼ cup butter

3 scallions, sliced

1 garlic clove, crushed

2 cups hot ham or vegetable stock

14-oz. can garbanzo beans, rinsed and drained

14-oz. can green lentils in water, rinsed and drained

1½ cups frozen peas

3 sage leaves, chopped (optional)

1 tablespoon olive oil

4 slices of prosciutto

salt and black pepper

1. Melt the butter in a large saucepan and cook the scallions and garlic over medium heat for 1–2 minutes, until softened.

2. Add the stock, garbanzo beans, lentils, peas, and sage, if using. Simmer for 5–6 minutes, until the peas are tender.

3. Meanwhile, heat the oil in a large skillet and fry the prosciutto until crispy, turning once. Drain on kitchen paper.

4. Puree half the soup in a blender or food processor until smooth. Return to the soup in the pan and reheat. Season to taste, then ladle into bowls and crumble the ham on top of each bowl.

Angel-hair Pasta with Olive Oil, Garlic, and Chili

What everyone remembers about the story of Rapunzel, of course, is the heroine's long golden hair, which first her adoptive mother, and then her princely lover, use to climb up into the tower where she has been imprisoned for her own protection.

Once again, it is well-nigh impossible to resist psychosexual readings of the tale: the doorless tower represents the mother's desire to keep her daughter safe and untouched, while the long, flowing hair, so flagrantly displayed, is a clear symbol of female sensuality—a meaning quite close to the surface in the modern phrase "to let one's hair down." Halting the development of sexuality is an impossibility, the tale seems to be telling us. Love and sex will always find a way.

This simple dish using angel-hair pasta—*capelli d'angelo*—is our small tribute to this famous fairy-tale heroine.

Garlic, chilies, parsley, and a good glug of olive oil create a bowl of pasta heaven with minimum fuss.

Serves 4
Prep + cook time 20 minutes

14 oz. angel-hair pasta

½ cup olive oil

4 garlic cloves, finely chopped

2 small red chilies, deseeded and finely chopped

salt and black pepper

handful of parsley, chopped, to garnish

grated pecorino cheese, to serve (optional)

1. Cook the pasta in a large saucepan of lightly salted water according to the package directions until al dente.

2. Heat the oil in a large heavy-based skillet over low heat and add the garlic and chili. Cook gently for 1–2 minutes until the garlic just starts to turn golden.

3. Drain the pasta and transfer it to the skillet with a few tablespoons of the cooking water. Season to taste and toss to coat the pasta in the oil. Transfer to a dish, sprinkle with parsley, and serve with the pecorino, if desired.

"White Snake" Stuffed Mussels

Although the Grimms set out to collect specifically Germanic stories, their net inevitably ended up trawling an ocean much wider and deeper—folk tales, after all, rarely respect borders, cultures, or languages. One such case is "The White Snake," the story of a servant who develops the ability to understand the language of animals after eating a morsel of white snake (cooked, of course!). The story—or some of its elements and motifs—can be found across Europe, while the association of snakes with the gift of "zoolingualism" is an extremely old one: in Greek mythology, for example, the seer Melampus gains this gift after two snakes lick his ears clean while he sleeps. It surfaces in modern children's literature, too: fans of J. K. Rowling's Harry Potter books will know that the young bespectacled hero can speak and understand Parseltongue—the magic language of snakes and all creatures serpentine.

One of the best-known episodes in "The White Snake" is where the servant, in order to win the hand of a princess, is set the task of recovering a golden ring tossed into the sea by her father, the king. Her wooer must either recover the ring or be punished by drowning. Earlier in the tale the servant has been able to help three stranded fish, and these now reappear to return the favor, giving him a mussel inside of which is lodged the golden ring.

The mussel recipe on the following page is delicious enough to win you a prince or princess, or indeed whoever you like, even without a ring.

Everyone pitied the handsome Youth, and then left him alone on the seashore. There he stood considering what he should do, and presently he saw three Fishes at once swimming towards him, and they were no others than the three whose lives he had saved. The middle one bore a mussel-shell in its mouth, which it laid on the shore at the reel of the Youth, who, taking it up and opening it, found the gold ring within.

The White Snake

For a quick but impressive light meal, go one better than simple steamed mussels by stuffing them with a mouthwatering mix of cheese, herbs, and walnuts. Be sure to discard any mussels that haven't opened during cooking.

Serves 4

Prep + cook time 20 minutes

2–3 lb. large mussels, cleaned (about 48 mussels)

1 cup bread crumbs

⅓ cup walnut pieces

⅔ cup butter

6 garlic cloves, chopped

juice of 1 lemon

2 tablespoons grated Parmesan cheese

2 tablespoons chopped tarragon

small handful of parsley, chopped

1. Steam the mussels in a large, covered saucepan until they open, then drain. Discard any mussels that do not open. Break off the empty half of the shells and place the mussels on a baking sheet.

2. Place the bread crumbs, walnuts, butter, garlic, lemon juice, and Parmesan in a food processor and blitz until the mixture starts to come together. Add the herbs and blend until combined.

3. Divide the herb mixture between the mussels, making sure each mussel is covered. Cook under a preheated broiler for 2–3 minutes, until the stuffing is golden. You may need to cook the mussels in batches if you cannot fit them all on a single baking tray. Serve immediately.

The Brothers Grimm Cookbook

Flounder, Flounder, in the sea,
Hither quickly come to me;
For my wife, dame Isabel,
Wishes what I dare not tell.
The Fisherman and His Wife

Wishing Fish and French Fries

Many folk tales are designed not only to entertain but to instruct, with a clear moral message much like that of a fable. This is especially true of the Brothers Grimms' tale "The Fisherman and His Wife."

In the tale, a poor fisherman who lives with his wife in a hovel captures a fish, which tells him it can grant wishes and begs to be set free. The kindhearted fisherman does as he is asked, without exacting a wish, but when he returns home and tells his wife what has happened, she becomes angry, insisting that he go back, recapture the fish, and demand a wish—to live in a luxurious house. The fisherman, against his will and conscience, does as he is asked, and the wish is quickly granted. His wife, however, is still not satisfied, and again and again insists the fisherman go back to the fish with ever more grandiose, not to say megalomaniacal, wishes. Eventually, the wife asks her husband to wish to become equal to God, and on returning home he discovers that the couple are once again living in their hovel, reduced to poverty, but perhaps happier for all that—the ending is somewhat ambiguous.

Give delicious fish and French fries a lighter, healthier twist. Here, the French fries are baked,
rather than deep-fried, and the fish coated in bread crumbs, instead of batter, and pan-fried.

Serves 6

Prep + cook time 30 minutes

2 baking potatoes, about 6 oz. each, scrubbed

4 tablespoons sunflower oil

2 tablespoons all-purpose flour

1 egg, beaten

1½ cups dried bread crumbs

14 oz. skinless chunky white fish fillets, cut into bite-size pieces

salt and black pepper

1. Cut the potatoes into thin sticks, coat in 2 tablespoons of the oil, and spread out over a cookie sheet. Bake at 425°F for 20 minutes, turning occasionally, until golden and cooked through. Season with salt and pepper.

2. Meanwhile, place the flour on a plate, the beaten egg on another, and the bread crumbs on a third. Dip the fish pieces in the flour, then the egg, and finally the bread crumbs, pressing firmly to coat.

3. Heat the remaining oil in a skillet and cook the fish for 5 minutes, turning occasionally, until golden, crisp, and cooked through.

4. Divide the French fries between paper cones made from waxed paper and top with the pieces of fish.

The Valiant Tailor's Whirly Sausage Rolls

"The Valiant Little Tailor" takes up the theme of the tailor and the giant (see page 126), but takes it in an altogether different direction. The tale begins in a similar way—a boastful tailor, who has managed to swat seven flies in a single blow, sets off to see the world wearing a belt advertising his prowess: "Seven at One Blow"—which everyone he meets takes to refer to grown men, not flies. Our petty hero, likewise, meets a giant, who proceeds to test him with impossible feats. Once again, the wily tailor outwits the giant, but this time, instead of meeting a sticky end, ends up in another story: it is almost as if the patchwork bedspread has been flipped over and the fairy tale gets to start all over again!

In the second part of the story, it is a king who sets the tailor a series of impossible tasks: if he is to marry the king's daughter and succeed to half the kingdom, he must kill two giants, capture a unicorn, and kill a ferocious boar (the story reads almost like a comic folk version of the "Labors of Hercules"!). Once again the tailor, who always has his wits about him, wins through . . . no hovering in the air for him, but a kingdom and a queen.

These scrumptious sausage rolls celebrate our diminutive hero, who kills the boar not by dint of arms but by well-practiced guile. Try eating as many as seven of these "beasts" and you'll rightfully be able to boast of your prowess as well: "Seven in One Go"!

A twist—literally—on the classic recipe, these mini sausage rolls, with their curly-whirly pastry casing, are perfect for picnics, in lunch boxes, or for a party. Served warm with ketchup for dipping, they'll be snapped up in no time!

Makes 12

Prep + cook time 30 minutes

7 oz. ready-rolled puff pastry

16 chipolata sausages

beaten egg, to glaze

1 tablespoon sesame seeds

1. Unroll the pastry and cut into twelve ¾-inch strips widthwise. Wind a strip of pastry around each sausage and place on a cookie sheet. Brush with beaten egg and sprinkle a few sesame seeds on top.

2. Bake at 400°F for 20 minutes until the pastry is well risen and golden and the sausages are cooked.

Pork and Apple Balls

Like the cow (see page 48), the pig was another mainstay of the traditional peasant economy—every prosperous cottage would have a sty beside it, where perhaps a couple of pigs were fed with kitchen scraps and fattened ready for slaughter. Preserved in the form of cured or smoked hams and spiced and herbed sausages, pork played a crucial role in the European diet; in Germany, it was from early on an iconic food, loved by everyone. No doubt the Grimms, too, liked their sausage dinners, perhaps featuring Bregenwurst, the cumin-and-mace spiced sausage of their homeland of Lower Saxony.

Something of the importance of pigs is reflected in the Grimms' tale "Hans in Luck," in which the titular, none-too-clever hero is very proud of the "fine fat pig" he has swapped for a cow and is driving along the road. He is only tricked into bartering it for a goose when he is told a local squire has had a pig stolen from his sty and that he will likely be accused of stealing it and thrown into a pond.

Here is a pork recipe that Hans could have made . . . if only he hadn't been such a fool!

Pork and apple pair very happily together in these juicy mini meatballs. They're great served as a snack, dipped in tomato chutney or your favorite relish, and can also be served with mashed potatoes and some crunchy green vegetables for a quick dinner.

Serves 4

Prep + cook time 20 minutes

1 small unpeeled apple, cored and grated

1 small onion, grated

2½ cups ground pork

1 cup bread crumbs

3 tablespoons vegetable oil

To serve

tomato chutney

cherry tomato halves

1. Place the apple and onion in a bowl with the pork and, using a fork, mash all the ingredients together well. Shape into 16 rough balls. Place the bread crumbs on a plate and roll the balls in the bread crumbs to lightly coat.

2. Heat the oil in a large heavy-based skillet and cook the balls over medium–high heat for 8–10 minutes, turning frequently, until cooked through. Drain on paper towels.

3. Serve warm with tomato chutney and cherry tomatoes, and provide toothpicks for dipping the balls in the chutney.

"I hate cow-beef; it is not tender enough for me [said Hans]. If it were a pig now—like that fat gentleman you are driving along at his ease—one could do something with it; it would at any rate make sausages."

Hans in Luck

Feast and Famine

The Grimms' tale "The Crumbs on the Table" tells how a rooster encourages his hens to go into a farmhouse to peck the bread crumbs from the table. The hens at first refuse, pointing out that their mistress, the farmer's wife, would give them a beating if they are caught, but eventually they give in to temptation. Sure enough, their mistress beats them and the rooster laughs at their discomfort: "Didn't I know it, know it, know it?" he delightedly crows. The tale is so short and seemingly inconsequential that we might easily miss the point(s): one of these is that, in a peasant economy, food is a scarce and valuable commodity and even a few stray bread crumbs on a table are to be treated with respect, not squandered.

Food shortages, hunger, and even famine loomed large for the poor in pre-industrial European societies like the Grimms'. Failed harvests due to poor weather or natural disasters always threatened production, while human-made misfortunes, most notably wars, hit both the production and distribution of food. Increasing population density, meanwhile, increased competition for scarce resources: the peasantry, even though their labor was vital for putting food on everyone's table, were often last in line when food was shared. Even in good years, food was hard to come by. By the eighteenth century, new crops and agricultural techniques had improved matters considerably, but nonetheless famine did not go away: in or just before the Grimms' lifetimes, there were significant famines in the Czech lands (1770–71), Saxony and southern Germany (1771–72), Sweden (1773), Iceland (1783), France (1788), and repeatedly, from 1804, in Austrian Galicia—variously caused by all the usual catalysts: poor harvests, natural disasters, wars, and plain bad management.

No wonder then that the specter of hunger haunts many of the Grimms' tales. In some, it is dealt with full on in all its horror. In "The Starving Children"—a tale included in the first edition of the *Tales* but subsequently excised—a mother is so famished that she goes mad and plans to kill one of her daughters. One of her offspring promises to find some bread, but acquires only enough to stave off the family's hunger for a very short while. The mother's madness returns and finally the daughters suggest that they will go to sleep until the end of the world.

This they do, and the mother, in her madness, wanders away never to be seen again. In other tales, famine is the "inciting incident"—as in "Hansel and Gretel" where a famine forces the woodsman and his wife to abandon their children in the forest.

Fairy tales, however, deal not only with the horrors of real life but also with wish fulfillment and consolation: if only, they seem to say, life could be different and food abundant and labor-free. Thus, for example, in "The Knapsack, the Hat, and the Horn," we find a magic table that lays itself with every kind of food; the cottage in "Hansel and Gretel" is made of cake and other sweet things; while in "The Raven" we find a supply of bread, meat, and wine that never runs out. Perhaps the ultimate expression of such fantasies of plenty occurs in "Sweet Oatmeal," in which a magic cooking pot produces oatmeal on command. Such fantasies were just that, fantastical, as every hard-headed peasant knows—the house made of cake turns out to be a witch's hellhole and the oatmeal turns the village into a swamp: anyone wanting to visit it has to eat their way through!

The Magic Cooking Pot

Phew . . . against all the odds—that tricksy, big-bellied wolf who tried to lead us astray in the woods, that grimacing hobgoblin who made us guess his name, that woman in the cottage with an unnerving penchant for cannibalism—we've safely reached our destination and we're just sitting down to a hearty dinner with our friends and family. The magic isn't really over, though, as Granny—who we have always suspected isn't quite what she seems (haven't we seen that glint in her eye?)—has been busy working wonders in the kitchen . . .

In this section, you'll find meals that will amply reward every hero and heroine who has come home a little tired and jaded after their day's adventures: paellas, curries, and stews; roast meats and pies; pasta dishes, and plenty of potato accompaniments. This is proper food for sharing, to sit down around the table for, to—who knows?—tell tales over: "Once upon a time . . ."

Garlicky Bean and Mixed Vegetable Roast

For many readers, beans can bring to mind only one fairy tale, "Jack and the Beanstalk"—one of the classic tales of the English-speaking world and the subject of many retellings, movies and, of course, pantomimes. The tale—at least in this English form—is absent from the Grimms' collection, but the humble bean still gets to play a starring role in one of their own stories, "The Straw, the Coal, and the Bean."

A woman is cooking a pot of a beans when perchance a straw, a coal, and a bean escape from their certain death in the fire and land on the kitchen floor. They become firm friends and decide to set off on an adventure. They reach a river and the straw offers to act as a bridge. The coal crosses first, but at the sight of the tumultuous waters below, takes fright in the middle, lingers too long, and sets light to the straw. Both are destroyed in the ensuing catastrophe (you can't escape your fate, the story seems to say).

The bean, seeing his friends meet their end, can't help laughing, until it bursts itself to pieces. Happily, a tailor comes along and offers to sew the bean back together. Ever since, the story tells us, with a glint in its fictional eye, beans have had a black seam.

This full-of-sunshine recipe is lovely served with crusty bread as a main course or as a side alongside slow-roasted lamb. If you have some, crumbling over a little tangy goat cheese or feta wouldn't go amiss.

Serves 4

Prep + cook time 55 minutes

1 green bell pepper, cored, deseeded, and cut into chunks

1 red bell pepper, cored, deseeded, and cut into chunks

1 yellow bell pepper, cored, deseeded, and cut into chunks

1 eggplant, trimmed and cut into chunks

1 zucchini, trimmed and sliced

1 red onion, cut into wedges

a few rosemary sprigs

a few thyme sprigs

4 tablespoons olive oil

4 tomatoes, cut into wedges

2 cups mushrooms, trimmed

4 garlic cloves, unpeeled

14-oz. can flageolet beans, rinsed and drained

2 tablespoons balsamic vinegar

½ cup black olives, pitted

salt and black pepper

1. Put the peppers, eggplant, zucchini, onion, rosemary, and thyme in a large roasting pan. Drizzle over the oil, season with salt and pepper, and toss until evenly coated in the oil, then spread out in a single layer. Roast in the oven at 400°F for 20 minutes until starting to soften.

2. Add the tomatoes, mushrooms, and garlic cloves and mix with the other vegetables, then roast for an additional 10 minutes until all the vegetables are tender.

3. Squeeze the soft garlic out of its skin onto the vegetables in the pan. Add the beans and vinegar and mix well. Return to the oven for another 10 minutes. Sprinkle with the olives and serve.

In a certain village there dwelt a poor old woman, who had gathered a dish of beans, which she wished to cook. So she made a fire upon the hearth, and, that it might burn the quicker, she lighted it with a handful of straw. And as she shook the beans up in the saucepan, one fell out unperceived, and came down upon the ground near a straw.

The Straw, the Coal, and the Bean

The Brothers Grimm Cookbook

"Six Swans" Nettle Pie

Sometimes, the Grimms' collection included tales that were clearly very closely related—examples of how stories morph across cultures and regions and from teller to teller. This is the case with "The Twelve Brothers" and "The Six Swans," in both of which brothers previously transformed into birds are able to change back again just in time and rescue their beloved sister from being burned at the stake as a witch (see page 130).

In "The Six Swans," six princes are turned into swans by their wicked stepmother and can only be transformed back again if their sister remains silent for six years and sews them shirts out of nettles. As in "The Twelve Brothers," the princess marries a king but, accused of witchcraft by her mother-in-law, is sent to the stake. She takes the nettle shirts to the place of execution, the swan-brothers swoop down, and she throws the shirts over them—their humanity restored, they rescue their sister from her fate.

Nettles have long been used to make textiles—with cotton imports sanctioned, German soldiers wore nettle-cloth uniforms in the World War I—and today are often billed as the sustainable "silk" of the future—so the princess's task is not so madcap as it might first appear. Nettles are also good to eat, as this recipe shows.

Be sure to wear gloves when handling the nettles and wash them well in cold water. If you can't find nettles, replace them with Swiss chard. This is perfect either hot from the oven, just warm, or at room temperature.

Serves 6

Prep + cook time 1 hour

10 oz. young nettle leaves, thoroughly washed and tougher stalks discarded

2 tablespoons olive oil

6 scallions, trimmed and finely chopped

2 tablespoons finely chopped dill

2 tablespoons finely chopped Italian parsley

1¼ cups feta cheese, crumbled

⅔ cup Parmesan cheese, grated

zest of 1 lemon

1 egg, lightly beaten

⅓ cup butter, melted

9 oz. phyllo pastry

salt and black pepper

1. Add the nettle leaves to a large saucepan of boiling salted water and cook for 3 minutes, then drain and allow to cool. When the nettles are cool enough to handle, squeeze as much water from them as possible, then finely chop.

2. Heat the oil in a large skillet over medium heat. Add the scallions and fry for 5 minutes or until soft. Take off the heat and mix in the chopped herbs, both cheeses, the chopped nettles, the lemon zest, the beaten egg, and season well.

3. Grease an 8-inch square baking pan with a little of the melted butter. Brush half the phyllo sheets with melted butter and use them to line the pan around the base and all the sides, leaving some of the pastry overhanging. Tip in the filling, then cut the remaining phyllo sheets in half, brush with butter, and drape over the top. Bring in the overhanging edges to seal everything in, then brush the pastry topping with any remaining butter.

4. Bake at 350°F for 30–35 minutes or until golden brown.

. . . on the road they passed a nettle-bush, whereupon the bride sang in a strange language—
"Nettle-bush! oh, nettle-bush
Have you forgot the day
When I cooked your juicy roots,
My hunger sharp to stay?"

Maid Maleen

Meatless "Meatballs" and Spaghetti

There is no Fairy Godmother in the Grimms' version of "Cinderella" (see pages 34 and 69). Instead, there is a magical hazel tree that, through the medium of a white bird, grants the heroine's wishes. Both the Fairy Godmother and tree, however, are in some sense incarnations of Cinderella's dead mother, who takes care of her daughter from beyond the grave. The episode of the hazel tree is especially moving, as the heroine finds consolation for her grief:

> *It happened that the father was once going to the fair, and he asked his two stepdaughters what he should bring back for them.*
>
> *"Beautiful dresses," said one. "Pearls and jewels," said the second.*
>
> *"And you, Cinderella," said he, "what will you have?"*
>
> *"Father, break off for me the first branch which knocks against your hat on your way home."*

So he bought beautiful dresses, pearls, and jewels for his two stepdaughters, and on his way home, as he was riding through a green thicket, a hazel twig brushed against him and knocked off his hat. Then he broke off the branch and took it with him. When he reached home he gave his stepdaughters the things that they had wished for, and to Cinderella he gave the branch from the hazel bush. Cinderella thanked him, went to her mother's grave and planted the branch on it, and wept so much that the tears fell down on it and watered it. And it grew and became a handsome tree. Thrice a day Cinderella went and sat beneath it, and wept and prayed, and a little white bird always came on the tree, and if Cinderella expressed a wish, the bird threw down to her what she had wished for.

Here is a dish, using hazelnuts, that commemorates one of the most moving moments in all of the Grimms' tales.

Is there anything more comforting than a big bowl of spaghetti and meatballs? Packed with vegetables, herbs, and nuts, these "meatballs" are so tasty that even committed meat-lovers will be clamoring for more.

Serves 4

Prep + cook time 45 minutes

1 tablespoon oil

1 onion, finely chopped

1 celery stalk, finely chopped

1 garlic clove, crushed

1 carrot, peeled and coarsely grated

½ zucchini, coarsely grated

2 cups mushrooms, finely chopped

1 teaspoon yeast extract

1 cup fresh white bread crumbs

½ cup mixed nuts, such as hazelnuts, pistachios, and blanched almonds, finely chopped

2 tablespoons chopped Italian parsley

1 tablespoon chopped rosemary

1 tablespoon whole-wheat flour

salt and black pepper

To serve

12 oz. dried spaghetti

11½-oz. jar ready-made tomato pasta sauce

handful of basil leaves

1. Heat the oil in a skillet, add the onion, celery, and garlic, and cook over gentle heat for 5 minutes until softened. Add the carrot, zucchini, and mushrooms and cook for 5 minutes until tender.

2. Remove from the heat and stir in the yeast extract, bread crumbs, nuts, herbs, flour, and some salt and pepper.

3. Roll into 20 small balls, place on a cookie sheet, and bake at 400°F for 15 minutes until golden.

4. Meanwhile, cook the spaghetti in a large saucepan of boiling salted water according to the package directions until al dente.

5. Heat the pasta sauce in a skillet over gentle heat. Add the cooked "meatballs" to the pan of sauce and carefully toss to coat in the sauce.

6. Drain the spaghetti and serve topped with the sauce and "meatballs," sprinkled with the basil leaves.

Pumpkin Coach Curry

Fairy stories mutate over the generations, reflecting changing tastes and audiences. Some versions, however, take a stubborn hold, refusing to move on or to evolve. This has been the case for "Cinderella," where it is Charles Perrault's 1697 romantic, soft-hearted version, "Cendrillon, ou la petite pantoufle de verre" (Cinderella, or The Little Glass Slipper), that has largely hogged the limelight, and certainly not the 1812/1819 version by the Brothers Grimm, in which any lingering romanticism is undercut by grotesque violence.

The sweet magic of Perrault's version ensured its longevity as a tale for children, as well as its immortalization by Walt Disney in the 1950 animated film. Here we find all the elements that we know and love today—including, of course, the glorious pumpkin coach—visualized as an airy globe with spiral, starlit wheels. Perrault's tale ends with universal forgiveness and happily-ever-afters, while the Grimms', in rather stark contrast, ends with the Hitchcockian pecking out of the stepsisters' eyes.

Fragrant, creamy, and spicy, this is a bowl of vegetarian goodness. Once you've mastered this easy recipe, play around with the ingredients—swap green Thai curry paste for the red or use a mix of sliced zucchini, carrots, and red bell pepper instead of the pumpkin.

Serves 4

Prep + cook time 30 minutes

1 tablespoon sunflower oil

1 tablespoon Thai red curry paste

4 cups peeled, deseeded pumpkin, cubed

1¾ cups vegetable stock

14-oz. can coconut milk

6 lime leaves, bruised, plus extra shredded leaves to garnish

1½ cups frozen peas

2½ cups firm tofu, diced

2 tablespoons light soy sauce

juice of 1 lime

To garnish

chopped fresh cilantro

finely chopped red chili

1. Heat the oil in a wok or deep skillet, add the curry paste, and stir-fry over low heat for 1 minute. Add the pumpkin, stir-fry briefly, and then add the stock, coconut milk, and the bruised lime leaves. Bring to a boil, then cover, reduce the heat, and simmer gently for 15 minutes until the pumpkin is cooked.

2. Stir in the peas, tofu, soy sauce, and lime juice and simmer for an additional 5 minutes until the peas are cooked. Spoon into serving bowls and garnish with shredded lime leaves, chopped cilantro, and chili.

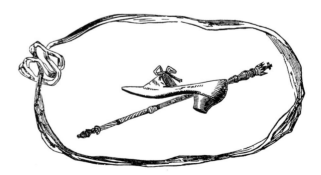

Gretel's Spicy Crab Curry

Of all the Grimms' tales food is most central to "Hansel and Gretel," a tale that begins with a great famine and ends in plenty. One of the more curious details in the story, however, is the crab claw that the witch feeds to the half-starved Gretel while her caged brother is being fattened up with all sorts of good things.

We may well wonder, if we were being picky, where the witch would get such an item, deep in a forest, perhaps hundreds of miles from the sea, and how does Gretel even eat such a thing? It's possible, of course, that she boils them up into a broth, but probably the very point of the crab claw is that it is inedible—the cruelest thing the witch could have given the girl to eat in this cottage where otherwise abundance rules, where literally everything and everyone is edible. In the meantime, presumably the crabmeat provided the witch and her caged protégé with some truly delectable dinners!

Crabs also turn up in "The Master Thief" (see page 112), where the hero fools the local parson and parish clerk into thinking that the Day of Judgment has arrived by tying lit candles to a sackful of crabs and letting them loose in the churchyard at night—pretending they are the souls of the dead scurrying about collecting their old bones. The Grimms—and their tale-tellers—had a wicked sense of humor!

The gentle spicing in this curry really enhances the sweet flavor of the crab. Serve it with basmati rice, pickles, spoons to scoop up the gorgeous broth, and plenty of paper towels—it's messy but fun to eat.

Serves 4

Prep + cook time 55 minutes

2 cooked fresh crabs, about
    1½ lb. each

3 onions, finely chopped

6 garlic cloves, finely chopped

1 tablespoon peeled and finely
    grated fresh ginger

½ teaspoon fenugreek seeds

10 curry leaves

1 cinnamon stick

2 teaspoons chili powder

1 teaspoon ground turmeric

14-oz. can coconut milk

salt and black pepper

1. Divide each crab into portions, by first removing the main shell. Next remove the two large claws and use a sharp knife to cut the body into two pieces, leaving the legs attached.

2. Place the onions, garlic, ginger, fenugreek, curry leaves, cinnamon, chili, turmeric, and coconut milk in a large saucepan. Season to taste, cover, and simmer gently for 30 minutes.

3. Add the crabs to the simmering sauce and cook for 10 minutes to heat through. Spoon into shallow serving bowls and serve immediately.

"Get up, you lazy thing, and fetch some water to cook something good for your brother who must remain in that stall and get fat; when he is fat enough I shall eat him." Gretel began to cry, but it was all useless, for the old witch made her do as she wished. So a nice meal was cooked for Hansel, but Gretel got nothing else but a crab's claw.

Hansel and Gretel

Golden Mountain Paella

In "King of the Golden Mountain," a peasant boy is abandoned in a boat, marries a princess, and becomes king of a magical kingdom. However, he is exiled through the treachery of his wife, but recovers his realm through the use of three magical implements.

The climax of the tale takes place in the king's former palace, where his estranged wife is about to remarry. Wearing a cloak of invisibility, he steals his wife's food and wine from under her nose at the wedding feast, until in her distress she runs from the hall to her bedchamber, where her husband confronts her with her betrayal. Then, returning to the hall, he commands the guests to depart and then, when they refuse, uses a magic sword to slay them all. He is once again King of the Golden Mountain.

Here we commemorate this particular wonder tale with a vegetable paella, golden with saffron and piled high as a mountain . . . well, almost!

Chicken and chorizo replace the more traditional seafood in this saffron-hued paella, which is best enjoyed outside in the sunshine in true Spanish style.

Serves 4

Prep + cook time 50 minutes

2 tablespoons olive oil

3⅓ cups boneless, skinless chicken thighs, cubed

1 onion, chopped

½ cup chorizo, sliced

2 garlic cloves, finely chopped

1 red bell pepper, cored, deseeded, and diced

1 orange bell pepper, cored, deseeded, and diced

2 celery stalks, diced

1 cup long-grain brown rice

3 cups chicken stock (see page 38)

2 pinches of saffron threads

½ teaspoon dried Mediterranean herbs

1 cup frozen peas

2 tablespoons chopped parsley, to garnish

1. Heat the oil in a large skillet over high heat until hot. Add the chicken, a few pieces at a time, until all the chicken is in the pan, and cook for 5 minutes, stirring, until browned. Remove the chicken with a slotted spoon.

2. Add the onion, chorizo, and garlic to the skillet and cook for 3–4 minutes, stirring, until the onion is beginning to color. Add the peppers and celery and cook for 2–3 minutes until just tender. Stir in the rice and the chicken. Add half the stock, the saffron, and dried herbs, season to taste, and stir well.

3. Bring to a boil, reduce the heat, and simmer for about 20 minutes, stirring occasionally. Add the remaining stock if the mixture becomes dry. Stir in the peas and cook for an additional 5 minutes or until the rice is cooked and the chicken is tender. Serve garnished with chopped parsley.

A month afterward, however, he went on his land to seek for anything he could find to sell, and there he saw a great heap of gold.

King of the Golden Mountain

Cabbage

Cabbages crop up several times in the *Tales*, such as in "The Rabbit's Bride," where a rabbit refuses to stop eating Mary's and her mother's cabbages until she follows him home. They also make brief appearances in shorter tales such as in "The Godfather," where a man comes across a house in which he passes several magical objects, including a set of bowls. He eventually finds the Godfather, who chides him for his apparent foolishness, insisting that the bowls were in fact nothing more than a pile of cabbages.

It is in "Donkey Cabbages," however, where the vegetable plays a starring role. In this tale, a good-hearted but foolish huntsman acquires both a magic cape that grants whatever he wishes for and the heart of a bird that, once swallowed, bestows a gold coin on its eater every day. Both cape and bird's heart, however, are stolen by a wily witch and her beautiful daughter—with whom, of course, the huntsman has fallen in love—and the huntsman ends up in a cabbage patch, where out of hunger he consumes a magical cabbage that transforms him into an ass. He then wanders to another part of the garden where, having munched on another cabbage, he is turned back into a human again.

The huntsman decides to use the "bad" cabbages to take revenge on the witch and her daughter. Disguising himself, he returns to the witch's castle and tempts the witch, the daughter, and their maidservant to eat some cooked cabbage. All are promptly transformed and the hero sells all three asses to a miller, who promises to treat the ass that was the witch's daughter well. The witch and the maid fare less well, and eventually the witch dies from her maltreatment. At last, the huntsman takes pity on the daughter and her maid and gives them some of the "good" cabbage, restoring them to their human form. The daughter is repentant, and the lovers can finally marry, to live happily ever after.

While the magical effect of the cabbages is a mystery, cabbages were traditionally associated with marital prosperity and fertility. Every peasant household would have a cabbage patch that could provide a family with a fresh, green head of cabbage all year round. The following recipes showcase just how good and versatile the seemingly humdrum cabbage can be. Don't be an ass, eat your greens!

Braised Red Cabbage

Christmas dinner wouldn't be complete without this richly colored favorite and it's a great dish to make ahead and reheat. For extra fruity flavor, you could add a generous ¾ cup sultanas at the same time as the apples.

Serves 8
Prep + cook time 2½ hours

1 red cabbage, about 3 lb., finely shredded

¼ cup butter

2 Spanish onions, thinly sliced

¼ cup brown sugar

2½ cups tart dessert apples, peeled, cored, and chopped

⅔ cup chicken stock (see page 38)

⅔ cup red wine

3 tablespoons wine vinegar or cider vinegar

1 small raw beet, peeled and coarsely grated

salt and black pepper

1. Put the cabbage in a large bowl. Cover with boiling water and set aside.

2. Melt the butter in a large heavy-based pan. Add the onions and fry, stirring frequently, over medium heat until soft and transparent. Stir in the sugar and continue to fry gently until the onions are caramelized and a rich golden color. Take great care not to let the sugar burn.

3. Drain the cabbage thoroughly. Add it to the pan with the apples, stock, wine, and vinegar. Mix well. Season generously with salt and pepper. Cover tightly and cook gently for 1½ hours, stirring occasionally.

4. Mix in the grated beet—this transforms the color—and continue to cook, covered, for an additional 30 minutes, or until the cabbage is soft. Adjust the seasoning if necessary, and serve hot.

Braised Black Cabbage with Cranberry Beans

Cavolo nero, or black cabbage, has a distinctive tangy, almost bitter taste. It's a robust green so is perfect for braising as in this recipe. Serve this Italian-inspired dish as a vegan main course and, for meat eaters, it makes a substantial side to go with a grilled steak.

Serves 4
Prep + cook time 40 minutes

3 lb. black cabbage

3 tablespoons olive oil

2 garlic cloves, thinly sliced

¼ teaspoon crushed dried chilies

14-oz. can cranberry beans, drained and rinsed

salt

1. Remove the thick stalks of the cabbage by holding the stems with one hand and using the other hand to strip away the leaves. Discard the stalks.

2. Cook the leaves in a saucepan of boiling water for 15 minutes until just tender, then drain thoroughly.

3. Heat the oil in a large skillet over low heat. Add the garlic, crushed chilies, and cranberry beans and cook for 5 minutes, then stir in the cooked cabbage. Season with salt and cook, stirring, for 6–8 minutes until the cabbage has completely wilted and absorbed the flavors. Serve immediately.

Fennel and Red Cabbage Slaw

Crunchy, creamy, and tasty, coleslaw is the ultimate summer salad, and homemade is definitely the way to go. Seeds add even more crunch in this recipe, enhanced with the sweet aniseed flavor of fennel.

Serves 4

Prep time 20 minutes

¼ red cabbage, shredded
1 fennel bulb, trimmed and thinly sliced
1 dessert apple, cored and thinly sliced
1 small red onion, thinly sliced
1 celery stalk, sliced
2 tablespoons sunflower seeds
2 tablespoons pumpkin seeds
5 tablespoons mayonnaise
1 tablespoon lemon juice
1 teaspoon Dijon mustard
small handful of Italian parsley, roughly chopped
salt and black pepper

1. Put the cabbage in a large bowl, add the fennel, apple, onion, celery, and sunflower and pumpkin seeds, and toss well to combine.

2. Mix the mayonnaise, lemon juice, and mustard together in a small bowl and season with salt and pepper. Add to the cabbage mixture with the parsley and gently toss together to coat in the dressing.

Carrot and Cashew Slaw

An unusual and healthy spin on this classic summer salad, spiced up with a little kick from the mustard seeds. Here, the traditional mayo is replaced with heart-healthy olive oil, and cashew nuts add protein, fiber, iron, zinc, and magnesium.

Serves 4

Prep + cook time 15 minutes

1¼ cups cashew nuts
5 carrots, peeled and grated
1 small white cabbage, shredded
1 small red onion, thinly sliced
1 tablespoon olive oil
2 teaspoons mustard seeds
1 tablespoon cumin seeds
2 tablespoons white wine vinegar
2 tablespoons cilantro leaves
salt and black pepper

1. Heat a nonstick skillet over medium–low heat and dry-fry the cashews for 3–4 minutes, stirring frequently, until golden and toasted.

2. Mix together the carrots, cabbage, and red onion in a serving bowl, then toss in the cashews.

3. Heat the olive oil in a skillet, add the mustard and cumin seeds, and cook until the mustard seeds start to pop. Stir in the vinegar and season. Pour over the carrot mixture and toss together with the cilantro leaves.

Chili Cabbage

Packed with goodness and flavor but low in calories, this is a great choice to pep up a simple grilled chicken breast or a piece of fish for a fast midweek meal. This also works really well with kale or spring greens.

Serves 4

Prep + cook time 20 minutes

1 tablespoon olive oil

1 garlic clove, crushed

1 large onion, chopped

1 lb. green cabbage, outer leaves and stalk removed, chopped

2 teaspoons lime juice

1 red chili, deseeded and chopped

salt and black pepper

1. Heat the oil in a wok or large skillet over medium heat. Add the garlic and onion, and sauté for about 10 minutes or until the onion is translucent.

2. Add the cabbage and stir-fry for an additional 5 minutes. Stir in the lime juice and chili, season with salt and pepper, and serve immediately.

Cabbage and Pepper Stir-fry

Quick and easy to prepare, this fragrant vegetarian stir-fry makes the most of crunchy, just-cooked cabbage. Enjoy it as a light meal, perhaps with some crusty bread, or serve it as a side dish.

Serves 4

Prep + cook time 20 minutes

1 tablespoon sunflower oil

2 garlic cloves, crushed

2 teaspoons medium curry powder

1 red bell pepper, cored, deseeded, and finely diced

½ green cabbage, finely shredded

3 eggs, lightly beaten

salt and black pepper

1. Heat the oil in a large wok or skillet until hot, add the garlic, curry powder, and red pepper, and stir-fry over medium-high heat for 3–4 minutes until softened.

2. Increase the heat to high, add the cabbage, season, and stir-fry for 5 minutes or until the cabbage is cooked but still retains a bite.

3. Stir in the eggs and mix well with the vegetables, then continue stirring until the eggs are scrambled and just cooked through. Serve immediately.

Hansel's Chicken and Leek Gratin with Bread-crumb Crust

One of the most iconic motifs in "Hansel and Gretel" is the bread-crumb trail. When the children are taken deep into the forest to be abandoned by their father and stepmother, Hansel drops a trail of bread crumbs along the way so that he and his sister can find their way back home. Soon after, the children discover that birds have eaten the trail and they are now hopelessly lost . . .

As with many elements in the Grimms' tales, the motif is an ancient one. There may be a distant connection with Ariadne's clue—or ball of thread—which the Greek hero Theseus uses to escape from the labyrinth after killing the minotaur, but perhaps a more relevant source is a *conte de fée* by Marie-Catherine d'Aulnoy, "Finette Cendron" (1697), in which the clever heroine adopts a similar strategy—using successively thread, ashes, and peas—to create trails home.

The bread-crumb trail—like Cendron's pea trail—seems doomed from the outset. Far better to have used the bread crumbs to stave off hunger pangs as the topping for this delicious gratin.

A lovely dish for when you want to add a little bit of luxury to a midweek meal. Serve with steamed green vegetables with a lemony dressing to cut through the creaminess.

Serves 4

Prep + cook time 1 hour

1 tablespoon olive oil

1 onion, chopped

1 garlic clove, crushed

4 leeks, trimmed, cleaned, and chopped

4 boneless, skinless chicken breasts, cut into chunks

1 small glass dry white wine

1 tablespoon all-purpose flour

1¼ cups chicken stock (see page 38)

½ cup heavy cream

2 tablespoons chopped tarragon

1 tablespoon English mustard

4 cups fresh bread crumbs

1 cup Gruyère cheese, grated

1. Heat the oil in a large saucepan, add the onion, garlic, and leeks, and fry for 3–4 minutes. Transfer the vegetables to a plate, add the chicken to the pan, and fry for 3 minutes until beginning to brown all over.

2. Add the wine and simmer until it has reduced by about half. Add the flour and cook, stirring, for 1 minute, then gradually add the stock and cook, stirring all the time, until the sauce has thickened.

3. Stir in the leek mixture, cream, tarragon, and mustard and season well. Transfer to an ovenproof dish, then sprinkle with the bread crumbs and Gruyère.

4. Bake at 400°F for 25–30 minutes until golden and bubbling.

The moon shone and they got up, but they could not see any crumbs, for the thousands of birds which had been flying about in the woods and fields had picked them all up.

Hansel and Gretel

Brier-Rose's Garlic Butter Stuffed Chicken

"Brier-Rose"—*Dornröschen* in German—is the Grimms' version of "Sleeping Beauty"—a fairy tale known since medieval times that reached its classic version in the volume of tales published by Charles Perrault in 1697. The brothers initially rejected the story as too obviously French, but ended up including it in their 1812 collection because the motif of the sleeping heroine rescued and wakened by a prince was found in Germanic sagas and poems. "Brier-Rose" was, however, dropped from later editions.

In this story, the good fairy (or wise woman in the *Tales*) seeks to soften the wicked fairy's curse on the baby princess by suspending time in the palace at the same moment the princess falls into her hundred-year sleep. The Grimms clearly took great delight in describing the slumbering court, as it is discovered by the daring prince:

When he walked inside the flies were asleep on the wall, the cook in the kitchen was still holding up his hand as if he wanted to grab the boy, and the maid was sitting in front of the black chicken that was supposed to be plucked. He walked further and saw all the attendants lying asleep in the hall, and above them near the throne the king and the queen were lying. He walked on still further, and it was so quiet that he could hear his own breath. Finally, he came to the tower and opened the door to the little room where Little Brier-Rose was sleeping.

As the spell is broken and the palace and its occupants return to life, we may well wonder what dish the cook went on to prepare with the chicken. Well, here's our idea . . .

Create a feast for friends with this one-pot chicken recipe that you can take straight from oven to table. Stuffing the chicken fillets with garlicky filling is the only fiddly bit—and that can be done ahead of your guests arriving—yet it looks so impressive.

Serves 4

Prep + cook time 1 hour

1 cup coarse bread crumbs

3 tablespoons olive oil

4 large skinless chicken breast fillets

2 tablespoons butter, softened

3 tablespoons cream cheese

2 garlic cloves, crushed

finely grated zest of 1 lemon

4 tablespoons chopped parsley

1 cup green beans, diagonally sliced into 1½-inch lengths

14-oz. can flageolet beans, rinsed and drained

¾ cup white wine

salt and black pepper

1. Put the bread crumbs in a flameproof casserole with 1 tablespoon of the oil and heat gently until the bread crumbs begin to brown and crisp. Drain to a plate.

2. Using a small knife, make a horizontal cut in each chicken breast to create a pocket for stuffing.

3. Beat the butter with the cream cheese, garlic, lemon zest, 1 tablespoon of the parsley, and salt and pepper. Pack the stuffing into the chicken breasts and seal the openings with wooden cocktail sticks.

4. Heat the remaining oil in the casserole and fry the chicken on both sides until lightly browned. Remove the chicken from the casserole. Sprinkle the green beans and flageolet beans into the casserole and add the wine and a little seasoning. Arrange the chicken on top.

5. Cover and bake at 375°F for 20 minutes. Remove the lid and sprinkle the chicken pieces with the bread crumbs. Return to the oven, uncovered, for an additional 10 minutes until the chicken is cooked through. Sprinkle the remaining parsley over the beans and serve.

Potatoes

When the potato was first introduced to Europe, it was initially met with widespread mistrust and suspicion—associated with illnesses, including leprosy and syphilis (the latter a possible New World import), lust, and witchcraft—and it was only from the mid-eighteenth century that it was widely established as a mainstay crop, becoming the ultimate, quintessential peasant food.

While the Grimms' *Tales* may have their origins in the medieval, pre-potato world, by the time of their compilation in the first decades of the nineteenth century, the potato loomed large in the contemporary diet and therefore had more than earned its place in the fantastic world of the *Tales*. It crops up several times in the *Tales*, such as in "The Poor Man and the Rich Man," in which an angel, dressed in torn clothing and looking for somewhere to stay for the night, is turned away by the rich man. The poor man, however, welcomes the angel and serves him potatoes that have been roasted over the fire.

Potatoes appear again in the tale "The Knapsack, the Hat, and the Horn," in which three brothers set out to seek their fortunes. One brother stops searching when he comes across some silver, the second when he finds gold. The third brother continues on his way, meeting several charcoal burners with whom he eats a potato supper.

In "The Master Thief," when the story's titular antihero turns up unrecognized at his peasant parents' home, it is his mother's potato dish that he asks for. A ne'er-do-well when he left, he has now made his riches by a life of thievery and looks every bit the aristocrat:

> The peasant stood up, went to the great man, and asked what he
> wanted, and in what way he could be useful to him? The stranger
> stretched out his hand to the old man, and said, "I want nothing but
> to enjoy for once a country dish; cook me some potatoes, in the way you
> always have them, and then I will sit down at your table and eat them
> with pleasure." The peasant smiled and said, "You are a count or a
> prince, or perhaps even a duke; noble gentlemen often have such fancies,
> but you shall have your wish."

For the Master Thief, potatoes have become a symbol of home and parental love, an object of nostalgia, the taste of his childhood . . . and, for a moment at least, a way back into his parents' hearts.

We can be sure that any of the following dishes would find favor with the Grimms' prodigal son.

Honey and Ginger Sweet Potatoes

Using honey enhances the natural earthy flavor of the sweet potatoes and caramelizes to a delicious stickiness that crusts the potatoes, turning a simple side into something sublime. For a vegan version, use maple syrup and replace the butter with extra olive oil.

Serves 6

Prep + cook time 1 hour

9 cups sweet potatoes, peeled and cut into even-sized pieces

¼ cup butter

1 tablespoon olive oil

1 tablespoon honey

pinch of ground ginger

salt and black pepper

1. Drop the sweet potatoes into a saucepan of salted boiling water and simmer for 5 minutes, then drain.

2. Melt half the butter with the oil in a flameproof dish and stir in the honey and ginger. Add the sweet potatoes and toss in the honey mixture. Dot with the remaining butter, then season with salt and pepper.

3. Bake at 350°F for 40 minutes, or until the potatoes are tender. Brush with the glaze in the pan and turn occasionally during cooking.

Unbeatable Roast Potatoes

Always the stars of the show, potatoes that are crispy on the outside and perfectly fluffy in the middle are impossible to resist. And the key to achieving great roast potatoes? Giving the boiled potatoes a really good shake around to rough up the edges and heating the oil until it is very hot.

Serves 4

Prep + cook time 1½ hours

3 lb. starchy potatoes, peeled

4 tablespoons sunflower oil or goose fat

salt

1. Cut the potatoes into chunky pieces, roughly the same size. Add to a saucepan of salted boiling water and cook for 8–10 minutes until the edges are just breaking up. Drain well, return to the pan, and give them a good shake.

2. Heat the oil or fat in a roasting pan in the oven at 400°F until very hot. Carefully add the potatoes to the pan and spoon over the oil evenly. Roast in the oven for 1 hour, turning once or twice, until golden brown and crisp.

3. Remove the potatoes from the oven, sprinkle with some salt, and serve immediately.

Potato Salad

*No barbecue or picnic is complete without
a bowl of potato salad. This version
includes crispy bacon for added flavor. For a
vegetarian version, replace the bacon with 2
ounces of blue cheese and add a handful of
roughly chopped walnuts for crunch.*

Serves 4—6

Prep + cook time 25 minutes, plus cooling

2 lb. new potatoes, halved

1 teaspoon vegetable oil

1 cup smoked bacon, cut into thin strips

6 scallions, finely sliced

¾ cup mayonnaise

salt and black pepper

1. Cook the potatoes in a saucepan of lightly
   salted boiling water until tender. Drain, rinse
   under cold water, and leave to cool.

2. Meanwhile, heat the oil in a skillet and cook
   the bacon until golden; drain on paper towels
   and allow to cool.

3. Put the potatoes, scallions—reserving a few
   to garnish—and bacon in a large salad bowl.
   Gently stir in the mayonnaise. Season to
   taste with salt and pepper, garnish with the
   reserved scallions, and serve.

Potato Dauphinoise

*Rich, meltingly tender, and with just a hint
of nutmeg and garlic, this French classic is
the undisputed prince of potato dishes. The
important thing is to get your potato slices
as thin as possible—using a mandolin or
the slicing attachment of a food processor is
the easiest way to do this.*

Serves 4—6

Prep + cook time 1—1¼ hours

1½—2 lb. evenly shaped potatoes, peeled and very
   thinly sliced

1 teaspoon grated nutmeg

1 garlic clove, crushed

1 cup heavy cream

⅔ cup Gruyère or cheddar cheese

salt and black pepper

1. Arrange the potatoes in layers in a well-
   greased ovenproof dish, sprinkling each layer
   with nutmeg, salt, and pepper.

2. Stir the crushed garlic clove into the cream
   and pour the cream over the potatoes.
   Sprinkle the cheese over the surface so that
   the potatoes are completely covered. Cover
   with foil and bake in the oven at 350°F for
   45 minutes.

3. Remove the foil and cook for an additional
   15—30 minutes, or until the potatoes are
   cooked through and the cheese topping is
   crusty and golden brown.

Mustard and Parsley Mashed Potatoes

Buttery, comforting, indulgent. Who doesn't love mashed potatoes? Choosing the right potato is key—waxy potatoes make gluey mash, so go for the high-starch varieties for the fluffiest, most flavor-packed results.

Serves 4

Prep + cook time 20 minutes, plus cooling

2 lb. starchy potatoes, such as Russet or red potatoes, scrubbed and quartered (leave unpeeled)

⅓ cup butter

1–2 tablespoons smooth Dijon mustard

1 garlic clove, crushed

1 large bunch of Italian parsley, chopped

dash of olive oil

salt and black pepper

1. Put the potatoes in a large saucepan of cold water, bring to a boil, and simmer for 15 minutes or until tender.

2. Drain well and, as soon as the potatoes are cool enough to handle, peel and return to the pan over low heat. Mash well until creamy. Add the butter, mustard, garlic, and a good sprinkling of salt and pepper, and continue mashing. Taste and add more mustard and seasoning, if desired. Finally, stir in the chopped parsley and a dash of olive oil.

Garlic Potatoes

A great garlicky side that's versatile enough to go with pretty much anything. Try it with the Nettle Pie on page 95 or with the Cranberry and Juniper Glazed Pork on page 129.

Serves 4–6

Prep + cook time 40 minutes

4 tablespoons olive oil

1½ lb. waxy potatoes, such as fingerling, peeled and thickly sliced

2 garlic cloves, finely chopped

salt and black pepper

chopped parsley, to garnish

1. Heat the oil in a large, heavy-based skillet over medium–high heat, add the potato slices, season with salt and pepper, and cook for 5 minutes until starting to turn golden.

2. Reduce the heat and cook for an additional 20 minutes, turning occasionally, until tender and golden all over. Sprinkle with the garlic and continue to cook for a couple of minutes. Serve sprinkled with chopped parsley.

Potato Wedges with Red Pepper Dip

Give your favorite side a healthy makeover with these seed-crusted wedges that are baked in the oven, rather than deep-fried. For an extra boost of goodness, they're served with a vibrant roasted vegetable dip.

Serves 4

Prep + cook time 50 minutes

1 lb. sweet potatoes, peeled and cut into wedges

1 lb. white potatoes, peeled and cut into wedges

4 tablespoons olive oil

1 tablespoon poppy seeds

1 tablespoon sesame seeds

1 teaspoon dried chili flakes

For the red pepper dip

1 large red bell pepper, cored, deseeded, and cut into 4 wedges

2 tomatoes, halved

½ teaspoon smoked paprika

3 tablespoons chopped cilantro

salt and black pepper

1. Drizzle the sweet potato and white potato wedges with 3 tablespoons of the olive oil in a large roasting pan and toss well, then sprinkle with the poppy seeds, sesame seeds, and chili flakes, then toss again. Season generously with salt and pepper, and roast on the top rack of the oven at 400°F for 35 minutes until golden.

2. Meanwhile, put the pepper wedges and tomatoes in a smaller roasting pan, then drizzle with the remaining olive oil and toss well. Roast on a lower rack in the oven for 25 minutes until softened and lightly charred in places.

3. Transfer the roasted pepper and tomatoes to a food processor, season generously with salt and pepper, and add the smoked paprika. Process until almost smooth but with a little texture still remaining. Spoon into a small serving bowl and place in the center of a serving platter.

4. Arrange the roasted potato wedges on the platter, sprinkle with the chopped cilantro, and serve.

"Make yourself at home: and though it is not much that we have, we will give it to you with all our heart." Then she placed some potatoes on the fire and, while they roasted, she milked her goat for something to drink with them. When the table was laid, the good angel sat down and ate with them: and the rude fare tasted well, because they who partook of it had happy faces.

The Poor Man and the Rich Man

Potato Skins with Guacamole

Potato skins are so easy to make and can be scaled up to feed a crowd. You can serve them with guacamole as here or top with grated cheddar cheese, chopped chives, and a dusting of cayenne pepper and place under the broiler until the cheese is golden and bubbling.

Serves 4

Prep + cook time 30 minutes

6 baking potatoes, washed

4 tablespoons olive oil

1 teaspoon Cajun spice mix

For the guacamole

1 avocado, halved, peeled, and pitted

finely grated zest and juice of
 ½ lemon

1 tablespoon sweet chili sauce

2 tablespoons finely chopped
 cilantro

black pepper

1. Prick the potatoes all over and cook for 10 minutes in a microwave on full power. Remove from the microwave, cut each in half, and scoop out most of the potato flesh, leaving a ½-inch border of potato next to the skin. (Use the scooped-out potato for the Potato Dumplings on page 122 or in another recipe.)

2. Cut each half into two wedges and place on a cookie sheet. Mix the oil with the Cajun spice mix and brush over the potato skins on both sides. Place on a cookie sheet and cook under a preheated broiler for 5–7 minutes, then turn the skins over and cook for an additional 5–7 minutes until crisp and golden.

3. Meanwhile, mash the avocado with the lemon zest and juice, season with pepper, and mix in the chili sauce and cilantro. Transfer to a small serving bowl and put it on a serving platter. Place the hot potato skins on the platter and use them to dip into the guacamole.

Potato Dumplings

Feel free to sub in chopped chives or some grated Parmesan instead of parsley to garnish your dumplings. They are also delicious with melted butter poured over. Whatever the garnish, serve them with a dish that has plenty of sauce or gravy—the Venison, Stout, and Chestnut Stew on page 131 would be ideal.

Serves 4

Prep + cook time 1 hour

1½ lb. starchy potatoes, such as
    Russet, peeled and quartered

1 egg, beaten

1 teaspoon salt

approximately 1 cup cornstarch

2 tablespoons finely chopped
    parsley, to garnish

1. Add the potatoes to a large saucepan of salted water and bring to a boil. Simmer for 15 minutes or until the potatoes are cooked through. Drain immediately, return the potatoes to the saucepan, and place on the still-hot stove for 30 seconds or so to encourage more water to evaporate.

2. Using a masher or potato ricer, mash the potatoes thoroughly, then set aside to cool, uncovered.

3. Mix the beaten egg and salt into the cooled mashed potato, then gradually add the cornstarch, mixing after each addition. You may need more or less of the cornstarch, depending on your potatoes. The mixture is the right consistency when you can form a dumpling that holds its shape. Roll the mixture in your palms to form dumplings about the size of golf balls.

4. Bring a large saucepan of salted water to a boil. Drop the dumplings gently into the water, then reduce the heat and simmer gently, uncovered, for 15–20 minutes.

5. Remove with a slotted spoon and serve immediately, garnished with the chopped parsley.

The Peasant's Wife thereupon went into the kitchen, and began to wash the potatoes, peel them, and make them into dumplings, as they were used to preparing them. While she thus proceeded with her work the Peasant invited the Lord to come and look round his garden, which yet yielded a little produce.

The Master Thief

Dorothea Viehmann's Roast Goose

Jacob and Wilhelm Grimm collected some forty of their tales from a German woman named Dorothea Viehmann (1755–1816), a tailor's widow living in Niederzwehren, Kassel, where she supported her family by growing and selling vegetables. She heard many of her stories from travelers when she was growing up as the daughter of a tavern keeper, but was clearly a skilled storyteller herself and, like all oral storytellers, had an astonishing memory for plot and vivid detail. No doubt, too, she changed an episode here and there to suit her own tastes.

One of the tales Viehmann told the Grimms is "The Goose Girl," in which a queen regretfully sends her daughter to a faraway land to marry a prince. En route, the princess's wicked maid usurps her mistress's place, swapping their clothes, and making her mistress swear an oath that she will not reveal the truth. On arrival in the faraway kingdom, preparations are made for the false princess's marriage while the true princess is made to guard the king's flock of geese along with a little boy named Conrad. When Conrad complains to the king of the strange, magical things that keep happening in the Goose Girl's vicinity, he asks her to tell him her story. Because of her oath, at first she refuses, only finally agreeing when the king suggests she tell her story from inside an iron stove, while he eavesdrops from the outside.

The princess is now restored to her royal position and the maid is punished by being rolled through town in a barrel lined with spikes—a typically gruesome Grimmian comeuppance.

No doubt, like many women of her time and class, Dorothea Viehmann kept a poultry yard and thought of her own geese every time she told this tale.

The Magic Cooking Pot

This is a centerpiece stunner if ever there was one. Enjoy it instead of turkey on Christmas Day or for any special occasion that calls for a truly spectacular main course. The stuffed apples provide a lovely fruity foil for the rich, juicy meat and the golden, crispy skin.

Serves 8

Prep + cook time 4¼ hours

11–13 lb. oven-ready goose, plus giblets

1 onion, halved

1 carrot

1 celery stalk

4¾ cups water

¼ cup butter

1 large onion, chopped

2½ cups dried figs, chopped

3½ cups fresh bread crumbs

2 tablespoons chopped parsley

2 tablespoons chopped thyme

1 egg

8 small apples, cored

16 whole cloves

2 tablespoons light brown sugar

½ teaspoon ground mixed spice

salt and black pepper

1. Put the giblets in a saucepan, discarding the liver. Add the halved onion, carrot, celery, and measured water. Bring to a boil, reduce the heat, and simmer gently for 1 hour. Strain the giblet stock and reserve.

2. Melt half the butter and fry the chopped onion for 3 minutes. Remove from the heat and add 1⅔ cups of the figs and the bread crumbs, parsley, thyme, and egg. Season lightly and mix well. Pack half the stuffing into the neck end of the goose. Shape the remaining stuffing into 1-inch balls.

3. Tuck the skin flap under the bird and truss it, with the wings folded under the body and the legs tied together with string. Place on a rack over a roasting pan. Roast the goose in the oven at 350°F for 2¾ hours.

4. Cut a thin slice off the top of each apple and stud with two whole cloves. Combine the remaining figs, the sugar, and mixed spice and pack into and on top of the apples. Melt the remaining butter and pour it over the apples.

5. Place the apples and stuffing in the oven 30 minutes before the end of the goose roasting time, basting the apples frequently with the butter. Test the goose to see if it is cooked by inserting a skewer into the thickest part of the thigh. The juices should run clear. If pink, cook for an additional 15 minutes and test again.

6. Transfer to a warm serving dish and add the spiced apples and stuffing balls. Keep warm.

7. Pour off all the fat from the roasting pan. Add 2½ cups reserved giblet stock, making up with water if necessary. Bring to a boil and season lightly with salt and pepper. Strain and serve with the goose.

As he sat eating, the smell of roast goose tickled his nose, and he got up and peeped about, and presently discovered that the landlord had put two geese into the oven to bake. Just then it occurred to him to try the wonderful power of his knapsack, and he went out at the door, and wished that two roast geese were safe within it.

Brother Lustig

The Giant's Boar and Cider Casserole

Fortune does not always favor the brave in the Grimms' tales and even the wiliest of heroes can come to a sticky end, as the story of "The Giant and the Tailor" shows. A tailor "who was great at boasting but ill at doing" decides to go traveling, and in a forest meets a rather stupid giant who takes him into his employment as a servant. The giant sets the tailor a succession of simple tasks—such as fetching water and firewood or shooting two or three boars for his supper—but the wily, lazy tailor shirks his duties by countering that he will bring back not just a pail of water but the whole well, not just a load of logs but the entire forest, and not just a brace of boars but a thousand. The giant is terrified, thinking he has taken on a powerful wizard as his servant.

The following morning, however, the giant is determined to test the tailor's strength and invites him to bend down a willow bough. The tailor, anxious to show off his prowess, holds in his breath to make himself heavier and just manages to succeed in his task. Unable to hold his breath any longer, he is propelled into the air by the bough as it springs back and, to the giant's relief, he is never seen again.

You may not have a thousand boars on hand, or even two or three, but a pound or two of good boar sausages will make this delicious casserole. Perhaps, that night, our giant sat down to a plateful just like this and thought, "Good riddance!"

This dish is packed with aromatic herbs and has raisins for little bursts of sweetness. Serve spooned over soft polenta. If you can't find boar, use venison instead.

Serves 4–5

Prep + cook time 2 hours

2 tablespoons all-purpose flour

2 lb. lean boar, cut into cubes

¼ cup butter

1 onion, chopped

2 celery stalks, sliced

4 garlic cloves, crushed

1½ teaspoons fennel seeds, crushed

1⅔ cups dry cider

¾ cup chicken or game stock (see page 38)

1 bouquet garni

⅓ cup raisins

salt and black pepper

1. Season the flour with salt and pepper on a plate. Coat the boar with the flour.

2. Melt half the butter in a large, heavy-based skillet and fry the meat, in batches, until browned. Use a slotted spoon to drain and transfer the meat to a casserole.

3. Melt the remaining butter in the skillet and fry the onion and celery for 5 minutes until softened. Add the garlic and fennel seeds to the skillet and fry for 1 minute.

4. Stir in the cider and stock and bring to a boil. Pour over the meat and add the bouquet garni and raisins. Cover and cook in the oven at 325°F for about 1¼ hours or until the meat is tender. Season to taste and serve.

Oxtail in Red Wine with Tomatoes

In "The Flail from Heaven," a peasant has a pair of oxen whose horns grow so enormous that he can no longer maneuver them through his farm gates. A butcher offers to take the oxen off his hands, in return for which he will give a Brabant thaler for every turnip seed the peasant can give him the following day. En route to the butcher's the next morning, the peasant drops one of the seeds, which, by the time of his return in the afternoon, has grown into a tree that reaches far into the sky. This the peasant decides to climb, and at the tree's top he reaches a field where angels are busy threshing oats.

At this moment, the peasant notices the tree beginning to sway and, glancing down, he notices that someone is chopping it down. He quickly weaves himself a ladder out of oat chaff, and having grabbed a hoe and a flail lying in the field, he climbs down and finds himself in a deep hole. Now it is the hoe that comes in handy, as he uses it to carve out a staircase up to ground level. And what of the flail? Well, this he uses to convince his listeners that his story is the God's honest truth!

It's a tale that seems to be making fun of listeners' suspension of disbelief—necessary for every kind of fiction. You've enjoyed the story so far, with its oversized ox horns, angelic farm laborers, and chaff ladders—this quite literally tall tale seems to say—but surely now you want some proof that all this actually happened? Any old piece of rusty farm equipment will do. Believe me—I'm telling you stories.

Oxtail releases a lot of fat, so ideally make the stew a day ahead, leave to cool completely, then refrigerate and skim off the solidified layer of fat before reheating. This is great served with the Mustard and Parsley Mashed Potatoes on page 117.

Serves 4

Prep + cook time 3¼ hours

4 lb. oxtail chunks

1 celery stalk, cut at an angle into 1½-inch slices

2 bay leaves

14-oz. can chopped tomatoes

1½ cups full-bodied red wine

1¼ cups beef or chicken stock (see page 38)

2 carrots, peeled and cut at an angle into 1½-inch slices

20 baby onions, peeled but kept whole

salt and black pepper

1. Season the oxtail with salt and pepper and put in a large, flameproof casserole with a tight-fitting lid. Add the celery and bay leaves, then pour in the tomatoes, wine, and stock. Bring to a boil, then reduce the heat to a barely visible simmer and cook, covered, for 2½ hours, stirring occasionally.

2. Add the carrots and onions. Re-cover and simmer gently for an additional 45 minutes, adding a little water if the sauce becomes too thick.

Cranberry and Juniper Glazed Pork

Perhaps the most disturbing of the Grimms' stories is "The Juniper Tree," sometimes translated as "The Almond Tree" (see page 157). It's a full-blown horror story involving child murder, decapitation, dismemberment, and cannibalism—an NC17-rated, Tarentino-esque bloodbath, far removed from anything that one might want to share with children. Even the bare outlines of the plot are unpleasant to repeat. A stepmother kills her unloved stepchild and serves him up to his father for dinner. His distressed half-sister, Marlinchen, gathers up his bones and buries them beneath a juniper tree. Soon after, a bird flies out of the tree and sings a lullaby to the townspeople.

To encourage the bird to sing its song again, a goldsmith, a shoemaker, and a miller give the bird, respectively, a gold chain, a pair of red shoes, and a millstone. The first two the bird gives to the father and Marlinchen, but the millstone it drops onto the head of the stepmother, killing her in an instant. Finally, the bird is transformed into the boy, miraculously restored to life.

The happy ending can scarcely make up for the gore-fest that has preceded it. The one saving grace is the image of the juniper tree itself—a tree that in European folklore was said to have hidden the holy family from Herod's soldiers during the flight into Egypt, which may explain its appearance here. Juniper berries, of course, have long been prized for their culinary and medicinal use, and this is what we celebrate here.

My mother she killed me,
My father he ate me,
My sister, little Marlinchen,
Gathered together all my bones,
Tied them in a silken handkerchief,
Laid them beneath the juniper-tree,
Kywitt, kywitt, what a beautiful bird am I!

The Juniper Tree

Mostly known as the prime ingredient in gin, juniper lends a welcome bold, citrussy, piney flavor to meat dishes. Here it is mixed with tangy cranberry sauce to glaze a succulent leg of pork. Serve this accompanied by the roast potatoes on page 113 and seasonal green vegetables.

Serves 6

Prep + cook time 2¼ hours, plus resting

3 lb. skinned, boned, and rolled leg of pork

2 teaspoons dried juniper berries

4 tablespoons ready-made cranberry sauce

2 tablespoons port

⅔ cup chicken stock (see page 38)

salt and black pepper

1. Place the pork in a large roasting pan and season with salt and pepper. Bake in the oven at 425°F for 30 minutes. Then turn the oven down to 350°F and cook for 1 hour more.

2. Meanwhile, crush the juniper berries using a mortar and pestle, or use a small bowl and the end of a rolling pin. Tip into a bowl and stir in the cranberry sauce and port. Season with a little salt and pepper.

3. Brush half the glaze over the pork and cook for an additional 30 minutes. When the cooking time is up, test to see if your pork is cooked by pushing a skewer into the thickest part of the meat. The juices should run completely clear, with no hint of pink. Pork should never be served rare.

4. Transfer the pork to a board or warm serving plate and leave to rest for 20 minutes.

5. Add the remaining glaze and the stock to the juices left in the roasting pan and cook over medium heat on the stovetop until heated through. Check the seasoning and pour into a small jug. Serve the pork cut into slices, with the sauce for pouring over.

Benjamin's Venison, Stout, and Chestnut Stew

Stories of siblings transformed into birds (and ultimately back again) abound in European folklore. Most often, the birds are swans, as in the Irish myth "The Children of Lír" or Hans Christian Andersen's literary fairy tale "The Wild Swans" or, indeed, the Grimms' own "The Six Swans" (see page 94). In another of their stories, "The Twelve Brothers," however, the sibling-birds are ravens, a bird of an altogether darker hue and reputation than the swan, often associated with the underworld but also considered guardian spirits.

In "The Twelve Brothers," a queen has rescued her sons from being murdered by their father, the king, by sending them to hide in a cottage in the forest. A thirteenth child, a girl, eventually goes to look for them and, for a time, lives happily with them in their cottage. When, however, the princess mistakenly plucks twelve white lilies from their garden, her brothers are changed into ravens and fly away—their only chance of being saved is if the girl can remain silent for seven years.

Despite her strange silence, the princess marries a king. Her jealous mother-in-law accuses her of witchcraft. Unable to defend herself, the young queen is sentenced to be burned at the stake, but is saved in the nick of time by her brothers, who fly down to the pyre, transform back into humans, and rescue her from the flames—seven years have passed!

The brothers' and girl's shared life in the forest cottage, before the brothers' transformation, is charmingly depicted in the tale. With her youngest brother, Benjamin, the princess stays at home to do the chores and cooking, while the others go out to hunt. At the end of the day they all sit down to a hearty stew.

This is the recipe for Benjamin's stew—taken straight from a raven's beak. Promise!

So they set forth into the forest, and shot hares, wild fawns, birds, and pigeons, and what else they could find. These they brought home to Benjamin, who cooked and dressed them for their different meals.

The Twelve Brothers

Nourishing and full of savory flavor, this is one to enjoy after a bracing winter walk. Make it ahead so all you need to do is light the fire, pour yourself a glass of something warming, and tuck in with gusto.

Serves 6

Prep + cook time 2½ hours

3 tablespoons all-purpose flour

2½ lb. venison, diced

¼ cup butter

1½ cups pancetta or bacon, chopped

1 small leek, trimmed, cleaned, and chopped

3 carrots, peeled and diced

2 parsnips, peeled and diced

4 garlic cloves, crushed

2 teaspoons chopped rosemary

2 cups stout

1¼ cups beef stock

1½ cups pack roasted and peeled chestnuts

1 lb. new potatoes, scrubbed and cut into small chunks

salt and black pepper

1. Season the flour with salt and pepper on a plate. Coat the venison with the flour.

2. Melt the butter in a flameproof casserole and fry the venison in batches until browned, lifting out with a slotted spoon onto a plate. Add the pancetta or bacon, leek, carrots, and parsnips to the casserole and fry gently for 6–8 minutes until lightly browned. Add the garlic, rosemary, and any flour left over from coating and cook, stirring, for 1 minute.

3. Blend in the stout and stock and bring to a simmer, stirring. Return the venison to the casserole, then reduce the heat, cover, and cook very gently for 1½ hours or until the meat is tender.

4. Add the chestnuts and potatoes and cook for an additional 20 minutes or until the potatoes are cooked through. Season to taste with salt and pepper.

The Wicked Queen's Liver Curry

When, in "Snow-White," the wicked queen, consumed by jealousy of her stepdaughter's beauty, orders a huntsman to take Snow-White to the woods and murder her, she also commands him to bring back her liver and lungs as proof (later versions substituted the more poetic, if only slightly less visceral, heart). When Snow-White begs for mercy, the huntsman stays his hand and sends the girl off into the woods. Instead, he kills a boar and takes its lungs and liver back to the queen, who proceeds to eat them (cooked, of course!).

Cannibalistic medicine was not unknown in pre-industrial Europe, so the queen's extreme behavior might be seen as an attempt to somehow co-opt her stepdaughter's youth and beauty.

Hopefully, this gruesome episode from such a well-loved fairy tale has not put you off your dinner. Unlike the wicked queen, you will be able to go to sleep after your meal with a light conscience.

Nutrient-dense liver has high levels of vitamins A and B, folate, iron, and copper, so it's a healthy choice for this spicy dish. If you like things a little milder, deseed the chili and opt for medium curry powder, rather than hot.

Serves 4

Prep + cook time 1 hour

1 lb. pork or calf's liver, thinly sliced

10 black peppercorns

1 tablespoon peanut oil

1 fresh red chili, finely chopped

1 onion, finely chopped

3 garlic cloves, finely chopped

1 teaspoon peeled and finely chopped fresh ginger

1 tablespoon hot curry powder

6 tablespoons chopped lemongrass

¼ teaspoon ground cloves

1 teaspoon ground cinnamon

10 curry leaves

1 tablespoon white wine vinegar

2 cups coconut milk

2 tablespoons each chopped mint and cilantro leaves

1. Place the liver in a small saucepan and add enough water to cover. Add the peppercorns, season with salt, and poach over low heat for about 10 minutes until the liver is just firm but still pink inside. Don't overcook it, or it will be tough. Remove from the heat and drain. When cool enough to handle, cut the liver into small dice.

2. Meanwhile, heat the oil in a large skillet over low heat. Add the chili, onion, garlic, and ginger, and fry gently for 10–12 minutes until soft.

3. Add the remaining ingredients, including the diced liver, and simmer gently, uncovered, over low heat for 20 minutes or until the sauce is thick.

Cabbages and Cows

The culinary fare eaten, enjoyed, and hankered after by the heroes and heroines in the Grimms' *Children's and Household Tales* reflects that of pre-industrial northern Europe of the eighteenth century and earlier. Readers quickly notice that a few staples recur with almost monotonous frequency: bread, butter, cheese, and roast meats turn up on cottage tables; stews and soups bubble away over hearths; fragrant sausages sizzle in skillets, attracting every dog in the neighborhood; apples dangle temptingly in orchards; cakes are offered as treats to ailing grandmothers, spoiled princesses, and hungry children alike; beer (and less often, wine) is offered to strangers . . .

This is the food of the German peasantry—when, that is, they were lucky enough to get it (see pages 88–89). Rich (and, some would say, stodgy) with nourishing fats and carbohydrates, it was made to sustain hardy folk through hard labor out in the fields and through long, perishingly cold winters (north-central Germany, where the Grimms came from, is roughly at the latitude of British Columbia and Newfoundland). Wheat, barley, oats, and rye were the staple cereals; root crops and members of the cabbage family were the stock vegetables; and cows, sheep, and goats were kept for milk, butter, and cheese. Local flavorings such as juniper berries, mustard, and parsley were preferred to exotic, expensive spices, despite Germany's vibrant trading traditions in Hanseatic ports like Hamburg, Bremen, and Cologne. Preserving methods such as smoking, curing, and pickling featured heavily, again owing to the land's brief growing season. To a large extent, it is these same characteristics that underpin German cuisine today, even though there is a wealth of regional variation in a country so large and diverse and many more cosmopolitan influences have gradually come into play: sausages, schnitzels, sauerkraut, pickled herrings, rye bread, and potato dumplings are enjoyed everywhere.

Occasionally, such food items get to play the starring role or are even the hero of a tale, and are not just confined to walk-on parts. In "Sweet Oatmeal," a magic cooking pot rustles up oatmeal on command but overflows when a mother does not know how to order it to stop, until

it swamps the entire village. And in "The Mouse, the Bird, and the Sausage," the sausage looks after the household's meals, including a final slither through the porridge to impart just the right greasy, salty flavor (see page 37).

The food of the *Tales* represents German food at its most *gemütlich*—cozy, comforting, and homely. In many ways, the food of the *Tales* represents a kind of antithesis and antidote to the *unheimlich* aspects of the typical fairy tale—a word that literally means "unhomely" but which also carries connotations of the uncanny, weird, or spooky. It's the food hankered after by the dispossessed, homeless children in "Hansel and Gretel" and with which the witch tempts them inside her home (which turns out to be a kind of anti-home, an *unheimliches Heim*—an unhomely/spooky house—so to speak—see page 99). It's the food missed by the antihero of "The Master Thief," who after years of separation from his parents and childhood home and despite his luxurious, ill-gotten lifestyle wants nothing more than his mother's potatoes, peasant-style (see page 112).

The Magic Cooking Pot

In a Single Gulp

We've said a lot about the food in fairy tales in the pages of this book so far, but little about the drink. But fairy-tale heroes and villains need to drink, too, and there are plenty of references in the Tales to the beer and wine that were long the standard beverages for peasants, townsfolk, and nobles alike. Something of the importance of beer in particular—drunk by everyone in a time when water supplies were often not safe—comes across in the Brothers Grimm tale "Frederick and Catherine." Here, the heroine, distracted by a dog that has run off with a sausage, forgets to close the spigot of the beer keg in the cellar and tries, unsuccessfully, to hide the fact from her husband by throwing flour over the spillage. Sometimes, fairy tales can be almost too much like real life!

For those times when you haven't disgracefully wasted, like Catherine, your stock of beers, wines, and cordials, the following section contains a few simple recipes to delight both your guests and you.

Spindle Tisane

It is a trope of all myths and fairy tales that, even if a character does their utmost to avoid a fated occurrence, it will happen anyway; indeed, the act of precaution itself can bring about the feared catastrophe.

So it is in "Little Brier-Rose"—the Grimms' version of "Sleeping Beauty." There, the king, on hearing that his daughter must fall into a deep sleep for a hundred years after pricking her finger on a spindle, destroys all the spindles in the kingdom. On her fifteenth birthday, nonetheless, the princess, wandering about the palace, comes across an old woman spinning in a distant tower. The girl is so entranced by the spindle that she goes to take hold of it . . . and the inevitable occurs. Sleep descends on her and, soon after, on the entire palace.

This soothing tisane will ready you, too, for a good night's sleep. We would all like to sleep as well and deeply as Sleeping Beauty (if not for a hundred years)—and to be just as beautiful, if not more so, when we get up from our bed the following morning as we climbed into it the night before.

This unusual but delicious tisane combines the sleep-inducing scent of lavender with sugar from the pear and honey to keep blood sugars stable to help you sleep all night long. Sip this about 30 minutes before bedtime and enjoy sweet dreams.

Serves 4

Prep time 5 minutes

approximately 2 cups boiling water

12–16 saffron threads

4 ready-to-eat dried pears

4 lavender stems

4–8 teaspoons runny honey

1. Pour 1 tablespoon of the measured boiling water into each of four heatproof glasses or mugs. Scatter three or four saffron threads into each glass or mug and leave to steep for 2–3 minutes.

2. Add a dried pear and a lavender stem to each glass or mug. Top up with boiling water, drizzle in 1–2 teaspoons honey to taste, and serve.

"What thing is that which twists round so merrily?" inquired the maiden, and she took the spindle to try her hand at spinning. Scarcely had she done so when the prophecy was fulfilled, for she pricked her finger; and at the very same moment she fell back upon a bed which stood near in a deep sleep.

Little Brier-Rose

A Grimm Gin Cocktail

The Grimms would have been familiar with the drink known as genever—the distilled malt wine flavored with juniper berries and other herbs first made in what is now the Netherlands and surrounding regions, including northwest Germany, the brothers' homelands. Initially drunk for reputedly medicinal reasons, it soon became a popular tipple among rich and poor. In England, the drink developed into the "gin" we know today—which, as "mother's ruin," caused a drinking craze (and accompanying moral panic) in eighteenth-century London, coruscated by satirical painter William Hogarth in his engraving *Gin Lane* (1751).

What are we to make, then, of the strange role played by juniper berries at the beginning of the Grimms' savage tale "The Juniper Tree"? There the mother dies after eating juniper berries from the tree in her garden and is then buried beneath it. Traditionally, the tree was thought to have protective powers, but here it seems much more ambivalent—a tree of both death and life. Is it too much to conjecture that the brothers—or storytellers—were playing on genever's more recent, darker reputation?

Our refreshing cocktail, more suited to a summer's garden party than the slums of Gin Lane, is an altogether lighter affair.

Also known as jenever and Dutch gin, genever remains a popular drink in the Netherlands and Belgium. Like modern gin, it is flavored with juniper, but is made in a pot still in the same way as whiskey. You can find it in specialty stores and online, or simply use gin instead in this recipe.

Serves 4

Prep time 5 minutes

ice cubes

½ cup genever or gin

⅔ cup apple juice

¼ cup lemon juice

¼ cup elderflower cordial

⅔ cup white wine

⅔ cup soda water

To decorate

apple slices

unwaxed lemon slices

mint leaves

1. Fill a jug with ice cubes, add all the ingredients, and stir. Decorate with apple and lemon slices, and mint leaves.

. . . she stood under the [juniper]-tree, it smelt so sweet, that her heart leaped for joy, and she could not help falling down on her knees; and when the sixth month had passed, the fruits were large, and she felt very happy; at the end of the seventh month, she snatched the [juniper berries] and ate them so greedily, that she was dreadfully ill . . . and she called her husband and cried . . . "If I die, bury me under the [juniper]-tree."

The Juniper Tree

Meanwhile the stranger, as soon as he found himself alone with his bride, pulled out the half of the ring and threw it into a cup of wine, which he handed across the table. She took it, and as soon as she had drunk it and seen the half ring lying at the bottom her heart beat rapidly. . .

Bearskin

Bearskin's Glühwein

"Bearskin" is one of the lesser-known of the Grimms' tales, though it contains many familiar elements: a man who bargains with the devil; a beastly form that disguises the "prince" beneath; and three sisters, only one of whom is virtuous.

A returning soldier is so poor he agrees to a pact with the Evil One: for seven years the soldier must go unshaven and unkempt and wear a bearskin a night, and in return his pockets will always be full of gold. If, during those seven years, the soldier dies, the devil can claim his soul; if he survives, he will be free to go his way. The soldier—now nicknamed Bearskin—follows the bargain to the letter but, despite his wild appearance, is careful to live a Christian life of kindness and charity.

One of the people he helps is an innkeeper, who in return promises him one of his three daughters in marriage. Two of the women run away in fright, firing insults at Bearskin as they do, but the third dutifully complies. The soldier promises to return in three years—when his pact with the devil ends—and, to plight his troth, gives his wife-to-be half a gold ring.

Three years pass, and the soldier is released, the devil giving him a makeover as a bonus. The now handsome, debonair soldier returns incognito to the innkeeper and asks to marry one of his daughters. The first two are now only too eager to be wed to the stranger, but Bearskin gives the other daughter a glass of wine into which he has dropped the other half of the gold ring: the truth is revealed and the happy couple marry. There is the customary Grimmsian sting in the tale: one sister hangs herself and the other drowns herself.

We, however, will backtrack to that moment of joy, truth, and recognition. The innkeeper has made up a jug of delicious Glühwein for his guest, made from the best wine in his cellar. The stranger gallantly offers a glass to his betrothed, still ignorant of his identity. As she goes to take a sip, she sees something glistening at the bottom of the glass . . .

A traditional recipe that will fill the kitchen with the heady scent of cloves and cinnamon. The brandy added at the end gives it an extra kick, but it's not essential. Take care not to let the mixture boil or you will boil off the alcohol!

Serves 6

Prep + cook time 20 minutes

2 lemons, sliced

1 orange, sliced

3 cups red wine

½ cup granulated sugar

8 whole cloves

2 cinnamon sticks

⅔ cup brandy

1. Place the slices of one lemon in a saucepan with the sliced orange, red wine, sugar, cloves, and cinnamon sticks. Simmer gently for 10 minutes, then reduce the heat and add the brandy.

2. Serve the Glühwein in small cups or heatproof glasses with the remaining slices of lemon.

Rumpelstiltskin's Mulled Ale

"Rumpelstiltskin" is one of the best known of the Grimms' tales, involving many of the classic features, structures, and stock characters of the fairy story. There's a beautiful maiden who is given an impossible task—spinning gold out of straw; a tyrannical king who, greedy for wealth, exacts that task under threat of death; and a supernatural being, an imp, who promises to save the heroine's life in return for a terrible payment (her firstborn child). The tale finishes with another common folkloric motif—a name-guessing task in which the potential victim discovers the name of the imp by a fluke of luck and is thus able to turn the tables on her persecutor.

Despite the heroine's eventual triumph, it's hard not to also have a sneaking sympathy for the imp, who, after all, helps the girl out in her moment of need (even if out of selfish motives). He is even prepared to compromise, allowing the new young queen three days to guess his name and thereby escape their dreadful bargain. There is even a scene in which, through the eyes of the queen's messenger, we catch glimpses of the imp in his cozy home. The messenger, in search of possible names, reports how, while out in the corner of the woods "where the fox and the hare say good-night," he comes across a little house. In front of the house burns a bonfire, around which leaps an "altogether comical little man," hopping on one leg and calling out:

"Today I'll bake; tomorrow I'll brew,
Then I'll fetch the queen's new child,
It is good that no one knows,
Rumpelstiltskin is my name."

With his baking and brewing, Rumpelstiltskin seems suddenly more of a domestic than devilish figure. Here, then, we imagine the poor imp nursing his wounded ego back in his cottage, comforting himself with a glass or two of his own delicious mulled ale.

Brimming with sweet spices, this deliciously warming party drink makes a great change from the more usual mulled wine. Pare the orange and lemon as thinly as you can, as you don't want to include any of the bitter-tasting white pith.

Serves 12

Prep + cook time 20 minutes

4¾ cups brown ale

⅔ cup brandy

3 tablespoons brown sugar

6 cloves

1 teaspoon ground ginger

pinch of grated nutmeg

pinch of ground cinnamon

peel and juice of 1 unwaxed lemon

peel and juice of 1 unwaxed orange

2⅓ cups water

orange slices, to decorate

1. Put all the ingredients in a large saucepan. Bring slowly to a boil, stirring all the time to dissolve the sugar. Turn off the heat and let stand for a few minutes.

2. To serve, strain into mugs or heatproof glasses and float orange slices on top.

Fundevogel's Roseade

The rose is a ubiquitous motif in European literature—from the medieval French allegorical romance *Roman de la rose* to any number of Renaissance sonnets to William Blake's famous poem "The Sick Rose" (1794)—a symbol of youthful feminine beauty, especially as the object of a man's love. It appears, too, in many of the Grimms' tales, including "Snow-White and Rose-Red," where the eponymous heroines live in a cottage planted with red and white roses, and "Brier-Rose," whose narcoleptic heroine is protected by a thicket of wild roses.

A rosebush appears, too, in the tale "Fundevogel." Here a girl and her adoptive brother—the title character—escape their father's wicked cook (who wants to boil the foundling alive) by turning into, respectively, a rose and the rosebush on which it blooms. The motif is symbolic of the children's enduring love for each other.

Eventually, of course, the children defeat the wicked cook by turning into a pond and a duck swimming on it. When the cook tries to slurp up the water, the duck holds her head under the water until she drowns. The children return home "heartily delighted," as the tale relates.

Perhaps they toasted their love with a glass of fragrant roseade, rather like this one.

Zingy lemons are softened by the floral notes of rose water in this refreshing drink—so pull up a deck chair in the shade and enjoy. Serve with plenty of ice and, for extra prettiness, decorate with edible dried rose petals or raspberries.

Serves 6

Prep + cook time 15 minutes, plus cooling

⅓ cup superfine sugar

7¼ cups water

4 unwaxed lemons, sliced

1–2 tablespoons rose water

ice cubes

1. Place the sugar in a saucepan with 2⅓ cups of the measured water and the lemon slices. Bring to a boil, stirring well until all the sugar has dissolved.

2. Remove from the heat and add the remaining water. Stir, then set aside to cool completely.

3. Once cold, roughly crush the lemon slices to release all the juice. Strain through a strainer into a jug and stir in 1 tablespoon of the rose water. Stir well, then taste and add more rose water if needed.

4. Chill until ready to serve, then pour into glasses and add ice cubes.

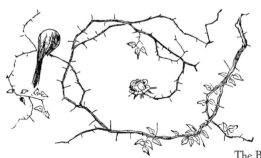

Apple Punch

Apples appear repeatedly in European fairy tales, just as they do in myth and legend. Sometimes their inclusion seems incidental—a piece of local color, so to speak—but more often than not it comes ready freighted with all the symbolism of two or three thousand years of human history, religion, and culture.

The half-poisoned, red-and-white apple in "Snow-White," given by the murderous queen to the innocent heroine, is a case in point. Even the most unworldly-wise could have read this without thinking of the temptation of Eve by the serpent in the Garden of Eden and the subsequent fall of man. Whatever the identity of the unnamed "forbidden fruit," in Western Christendom it had long been envisaged as an apple, if only for a pun based on the near-homophonic Latin words for "apple" and "evil"— *malus*. By eating the "forbidden fruit," Adam and Eve gained knowledge of both good and evil.

Suddenly, the wicked queen's gift and Snow-White's acceptance of it appear in a new light: from a Christian perspective, not even the best of us can escape the doom of humankind; even Snow-White must fall!

That said, we very much hope that you will be able to make, share, and drink this apple punch without worrying too much about the symbolic ramifications!

This nonalcoholic crowd-pleaser uses sugar syrup. You can buy it, or make your own by simply bringing equal quantities of superfine sugar and water to a boil in a saucepan, stirring constantly, then boil for 1–2 minutes without stirring. It will keep in a sterilized bottle in the refrigerator for up to two months.

Serves 25–30

Prep time 5 minutes

½ cup sugar syrup

1⅓ cups lemon juice

3⅔ cups apple juice

ice cubes

10 cups ginger ale

unwaxed orange slices, to decorate

1. Stir together the sugar syrup, lemon, and apple juices in a large chilled jug. Add the ice cubes and pour in the ginger ale.

2. Decorate with orange slices and serve.

Vivid Symbols

Drops of red blood on whitest snow; an apple half green, half red; an old gnarled juniper tree heavy with berries . . . the bare-bones nature of fairy tales—the simple, repetitive narratives, the stock characters, the recurring or multiplying motifs—mean that their symbolic or imagistic content often seems very close to the surface, vivid before the eye. The Grimm brothers, like the Romantic writers of literary fairy tales such as Ludwig Tieck (1773–1853) and Clemens Brentano (1778–1842), were more than aware of this, as, of course, were their readers. Since medieval times, oral storytelling of every kind had used conventional Christian or folkloric imagery that everyone, literate or not, could understand—much as they might grasp an image in a religious painting or in a stained-glass window. It was from this deep well of symbols that fairy tales draw upon.

In a tale like "The Girl without Hands," where the heroine eats an apple directly from a tree, readers could not fail to be reminded of the temptation of Eve with the fruit from the Tree of Knowledge (popularly an apple) in the Garden of Eden. Biblical stories in particular were always uppermost in people's minds, so that anything—an animal, tree, or food item—might easily be understood or interpreted in a Christian light. Mentions of bread and wine, for example, would inevitably summon up the Eucharist or any number of biblical stories or parables. Such symbolism may not always be quite so obvious or immediate to us today, when many of us are far less versed in Scripture.

In other ways, however, the symbolic interpretation of fairy tales, especially those of the Grimms, extended and deepened in the twentieth century with the development of psychoanalysis. Both its two great progenitors, the Austrian Sigmund Freud (1856–1939) and the Swiss Carl Jung (1875–1961), were German speakers and familiar with the Grimms' tales since childhood. Freud believed that fairy tales, much like dreams, could be used in psychoanalytic therapy: a subject's preoccupation with a particular fairy tale read or told to them in childhood could be used to understand and thus defuse their sexual neuroses. Thus, the patient Freud called "Wolf Man"—Sergei Pankejeff—was haunted by a picture of the predatory wolf in "Little Red Cap" he had seen as a child in a book of Grimms' tales. This Freud related to Pankejeff's terrifying dream of six white wolves sitting in a walnut tree outside his bedroom window—a scene that itself has the hallucinogenic quality of a fairy tale—and eventually to what Freud understood to be the trauma of the young boy witnessing his parents having sex.

For Jung, fairy stories provided insights into the "Collective Unconscious"—the shared psychological bedrock shared by all humankind—and into the archetypes that were rooted there—innate universal symbols relating to primal instincts such as the Mother, the Maiden, the Hero, and the Old Man—and that can be closely related to the simplified, stock characters of fairy tales.

Such insights could be used not only to understand patients but also to understand the fairy tales themselves. Such a study was systematically undertaken by another Austrian psychologist, Bruno Bettelheim (1903–90), who in *The Uses of Enchantment* (1976) decoded fairy tales using Freudian psychology. For Bettelheim, fairy tales, perhaps especially those of the Brothers Grimm, addressed many potentially traumatic issues—sex, death, grief, abandonment—but allowed younger readers to explore and come to grips with them in a safe, distanced way.

Happily Ever Afters

Culinarily speaking, there can be no real "happily ever after" unless a main course is followed by a dessert. This, many would argue, is where the real enchantment of a meal begins and ends, where all the woes of the world—the wolves and the warlocks of our everyday lives—can be transformed, if only for a few moments, to sweetness and light. Desserts and cakes are undoubtedly the true alchemy of the kitchen. Few can resist their magic.

So what marvels does our Fairy Godmother have in store for us, her much petted protégés? There are creations that could grace Sleeping Beauty's palace wedding banquet, from a strawberry sorbet to frosted grapes, but also homelier confections that you might come across, if you're lucky, in a woodman's cottage, Christmas Stollen and chocolate log. The pièce de résistance, though, is the Gingerbread House. That strange, terrifying cottage in the woods today? Well, you get it to eat it, after all. . .

The Three Little Men's Strawberry Sorbet

Wicked stepmothers abound, but rarely flourish, in fairy tales, including those by the Grimms. There are famous examples in "Aschenputtel," "Hansel and Gretel," and "Snow-White" (see pages 54, 108, and 151), but also in many other, lesser-known tales. Such women are uniformly shown as jealous of the first wife's children, greedy for the rights of their own (from this perspective, they are "good" mothers!), and murderous tyrants of their households, utterly eclipsing their weakly husbands who give in to their every whim. Interestingly, in the first versions of "Hansel and Gretel" and "Snow-White" the Grimms made the evil mother the hero's and heroine's biological mother, not stepmother, and only changed this in later editions.

In *The Uses of Enchantment* (1976), the Austrian-born psychologist Bruno Bettelheim argued that the fairy-tale stepmother was a symbolic means by which children were able to accept that the mother they loved might also have hateful aspects of her personality. However, cultural historians have also suggested that the wicked stepmother, to a degree, reflected the challenging role a second wife had in societies where women often died young in childbirth, where many men remarried, and where inheritance was subsequently fiercely fought over.

In the Grimms' tales, especially and inventively wicked is the stepmother of "The Three Little Men in the Wood," who, in the depths of winter, sends her loathed stepdaughter out into the woods in a paper dress to find wild strawberries— effectively a death sentence. With the help of the "three little men," or gnomes, however, the kindly stepdaughter is able to achieve her task. The familial struggle continues, however—though there's no prizes for guessing that it is the stepdaughter who ultimately triumphs and the stepmother who meets a typically gruesome end: in a barrel rolled down a hill into a river. *Plus ça change . . .*

What did the wicked stepmother do with those winter strawberries, we wonder. Why, make this delicious sorbet, of course!

Using just a few ingredients, this intensely flavored and bright-hued sorbet is super easy—
no ice-cream machine needed. Once you've nailed the method, experiment with other
flavors such as raspberry, peach, pineapple, and melon.

Serves 6

Prep time 15 minutes, plus
freezing

5 cups strawberries, hulled and
roughly chopped

⅔ cup superfine sugar

juice of 1 lemon

1¼ cups boiling water

1. Add the strawberries, superfine sugar, and lemon juice to a bowl and pour over the measured boiling water. Set aside to cool.

2. Once the mixture has cooled, blitz in a food processor until smooth, then push the puree through a strainer.

3. Pour the liquid into a freezerproof container and cover with plastic wrap. Freeze until frozen around the edges and slushy in the middle. Use a fork to break up the ice into smaller crystals. Return the container to the freezer.

4. Repeat the breaking-up process every 30 minutes, at least three times, until the sorbet is completely frozen and the texture of snow. Scoop into glasses or small bowls and serve.

Once in winter, when everything was frozen as hard as a stone, and the hills and valleys were covered with snow, the woman made a dress of paper, called her stepdaughter, and said, "Here, put this dress on and go out into the woods and fetch me a basketful of strawberries. I have a longing for some."

The Three Little Men in the Wood

Snow White's Red-and-White Linzer Cookies

The Brothers Grimm had an eye for vivid, haunting detail. The story of "Snow-White" begins with a childless queen sitting sewing at an open window in the midst of winter. She pricks herself with her needle and three drops of blood fall onto the snow that has itself fallen onto the black window ledge. The striking color contrast leads her to exclaim: "How I wish that I had a daughter that had skin as white as snow, lips as red as blood, and hair as black as ebony." A while later, the queen gives birth to a daughter whom she names Snow-White, but herself dies in childbirth.

The symbolism of white and red is complex and ancient. In classical mythology and poetry it was often associated with sex, love, and death: the maiden goddess Persephone, for example, is picking red poppies and white lilies when she is abducted by Hades, lord of the underworld. In the medieval German epic *Parzifal* by Wolfram von Eschenbach (c. 1160/80–c. 1220), the hero is reminded of his beloved wife when he sees blood on snow—that of a goose that has been wounded by a falcon.

Such resonances seem to be present in the Grimms' tale, where the red–white contrast recurs in the poisoned apples given to Snow-White by her evil stepmother: while the white half is harmless, the red half has been spiked with poison. Snow-White—echoing Persephone's descent into the underworld and eventual return with spring—takes a bite of the red half and falls into a deathlike state, from which she is rescued only when the piece of poisoned apple is dislodged from her throat when she is being carried in a glass coffin.

"What! Are you afraid of it?" cried the old woman; "There, see, will cut the apple in halves: do you eat the red cheeks and I will eat the core." (The apple was so artfully made that the red cheeks alone were poisoned.) Snow-White very much wished for the beautiful apple, and when she saw the woman eating the core she could no longer resist, but, stretching out her hand took the poisoned part.

Scarcely had she placed a piece in her mouth when she fell down dead upon the ground. Then the Queen, looking at her with glittering eyes, and laughing bitterly, exclaimed, "White as snow, red as blood, black as ebony! This time the Dwarfs cannot reawaken you."

Little Snow-White

A stunning color combination of pure white with dark red, these melt-in-the-mouth cookies are as pretty as a picture. For an orange and peach version, replace the lemon zest with orange zest and use peach preserves to sandwich the cookies together.

Makes 16

Prep + cook time 50 minutes, plus cooling

⅓ cup hazelnuts

2 cups all-purpose flour, plus extra for dusting

⅓ cup superfine sugar

⅔ cup butter, diced

finely grated zest of ½ lemon

1 egg yolk

4 tablespoons seedless raspberry preserves

sifted confectioners' sugar, for dusting

1. Grind the hazelnuts very finely in a blender or coffee grinder. Set aside.

2. Put the flour and sugar in a mixing bowl or a food processor. Add the butter and rub in with your fingertips or process until the mixture resembles fine bread crumbs. Stir in the ground hazelnuts and lemon zest, then mix in the egg yolk, and bring the mixture together with your hands to form a firm dough.

3. Knead lightly, then roll out half of the dough on a lightly floured surface until ½ inch thick. Stamp out 2¼-inch circles using a fluted round cookie cutter. Transfer to an ungreased cookie sheet. Use a small heart- or star-shaped cookie cutter to remove 1-inch hearts or stars from the middle of half of the cookies.

4. Bake the first cookies at 350°F for about 8 minutes, until pale golden brown, then repeat for the remaining dough.

5. Leave the cookies to harden for 1–2 minutes, then transfer to a wire rack to cool.

6. Divide the preserves evenly among the centers of the whole cookies and spread thickly, leaving a border of cookie showing. Cover with the hole-cut cookies, dust with a little sifted confectioners' sugar, and leave to cool completely before serving.

Stollen

Christmas-themed fairy tales are a rarity in the Grimms' oeuvre: an exception is the heartwarming "The Shoemaker and the Elves."

A pious shoemaker is so poor that he has only enough leather to make one last pair of shoes. Leaving the unsewn parts on his workbench, the shoemaker and his wife say their prayers and go to bed. In the morning, they discover that the shoes have been finished and in the most exquisite fashion. The shoemaker is able to sell the shoes at a higher than normal price and his business quickly begins to prosper as, every morning, more and more pairs of shoes appear, all beautifully stitched and finished.

One night, just before Christmas, the shoemaker and his wife decide to find out who is helping them: hiding in a dark corner of the workshop, they keep watch, and soon two little "elves"—the German is *Wichtelmänner* ("wight-men")—appear and begin busying themselves with the unmade shoes. The following day the shoemaker and his wife decide to show the kindly elves their gratitude—working the whole day long, the shoemaker makes the elves each a pair of shoes and the shoemaker's wife sews each of them a new suit of clothes. That night they leave out their gifts and once again hide in the dark corner. The elves delightedly try on the clothes and shoes and leap away out of the house, never to be seen again. The shoemaker's business, however, continues to prosper.

We might well imagine the shoemaker's wife also baking the elves the traditional yeasted Christmas cake known as Stollen, rich of fruit and marzipan. If the elves had tasted a slice or two of this, they might never have gone away!

More a fruit bread than a cake, this marzipan-filled delight is a German Christmas classic. It's traditionally dusted liberally with confectioners' sugar to create a snowlike layer, reminiscent of winter landscapes, so be sure to use plenty.

Serves 12

Prep + cook time 1 hour, plus
   proofing

3 tablespoons salted butter, plus
   extra for greasing

1½ cups white bread flour, plus
   extra for dusting

1½ teaspoons active dry yeast

½ teaspoon ground mixed spice

2 tablespoons superfine sugar

⅓ cup warm milk

½ cup golden raisins

¼ cup chopped almonds

¼ cup chopped candied peel

½ cup marzipan

confectioners' sugar, for dusting

1. Grease a large loaf pan with a base measurement of about 10 x 4 inches.

2. Put the flour, yeast, mixed spice, and sugar in a bowl. Melt 2 tablespoons of the butter, mix with the milk, and add to the bowl. Mix with a round-bladed knife to make a soft but not sticky dough.

3. Turn out onto a lightly floured surface and knead for 10 minutes until smooth and elastic. (Alternatively, use a freestanding mixer with a dough hook and knead for 5 minutes.)

4. Place in a lightly oiled bowl, cover with plastic wrap, and leave to rise in a warm place for about 1½ hours or until doubled in size.

5. Turn the dough out onto a floured surface and knead in the raisins, almonds, and candied peel. Cover loosely with a clean dish towel and leave to rest for 10 minutes.

6. Roll out the dough on a floured surface to a 10 x 8-inch rectangle. Roll the marzipan under the palms of your hands to form a log shape about 9 inches long and flatten to about ¼ inch thick. Lay the marzipan down the length of the dough, slightly to one side, and fold the rest of the dough over it. Transfer to the loaf pan and press down gently.

7. Cover loosely with oiled plastic wrap and leave to rise in a warm place for about 30 minutes until slightly risen. Remove the plastic wrap.

8. Bake at 425°F for 25 minutes until risen and golden. Leave for 5 minutes, then turn out of the pan, place on a wire rack, cover with a sheet of foil, and place a weight on top to keep the Stollen compact while cooling. Melt the remaining butter and brush over the Stollen. Dust generously with confectioners' sugar.

Apple and Almond Pie

In many Victorian versions or translations of the story "The Juniper Tree," the original Low German title "Von dem Machandelboom" was rendered as "The Almond Tree." Quite why the change was made isn't clear, although it may be simply a question of mistranslation: the translator may have been unfamiliar with the nonstandard Low German *Machandelboom* and mistaken it for *Mandelbaum*, which does indeed mean "almond tree." The particular species of the tree seems in any case of little importance, since the tree serves more broadly simply as a symbol for birth, death, and resurrection.

The story begins under a tree, where a childless woman cuts her finger while paring an apple and wishes for a child "as red as blood, and as white as snow!" It is under the tree that the same woman, who has died in childbirth, is buried and where the bones of her boy are likewise hidden by his grieving half-sister. And it is from the tree, finally, that the beautiful bird arises who will eventually transform back into the lost boy.

Here's a dessert that commemorates the tale's opening poignant moment: the mother-to-be paring an apple beneath an almond tree.

Serve this with vanilla ice cream or, for a indulgent treat, with homemade chocolate sauce: melt ⅔ cup chopped dark chocolate, ¼ cup diced unsalted butter, and 1 tablespoon light corn syrup together in a saucepan over low heat.

Serves 8

Prep + cook time 1¼ hours, plus chilling

16 oz. chilled ready-made or homemade piecrust

a little flour, for dusting

½ cup unsalted butter, softened

½ cup superfine sugar

1¼ cups ground almonds

2 eggs, lightly beaten

1 tablespoon lemon juice

3 ripe apples, peeled, cored, and thickly sliced

⅓ cup slivered almonds

confectioners' sugar, for dusting

1. Roll out the piecrust on a lightly floured surface and then lift it over a rolling pin and drape into a 10-inch loose-bottomed pie pan. Press over the base and up the sides of the pan with your fingertips. Trim off the excess piecrust by pressing with the rolling pin or using a small knife. Prick the base with a fork and chill for 30 minutes.

2. Line with nonstick baking paper, add pie weights, and bake at 375°F for 15 minutes. Remove the baking paper and pie weights and bake for an additional 5–10 minutes until the piecrust is crisp and golden. Leave to cool completely.

3. Beat the butter, sugar, and ground almonds together until smooth, then beat in the eggs and lemon juice.

4. Arrange the apple slices over the piecrust and carefully spread the almond mixture on top. Sprinkle with the slivered almonds and bake for 30 minutes until the topping is golden and firm. Remove from the oven and leave to cool.

5. Dust the pie with sifted confectioners' sugar and serve in wedges.

Then the almond-tree began to move, and the boughs spread out quite wide, and then went back again; just as when one is very much pleased and claps with the hands.

The Almond Tree (or The Juniper Tree)

The Poor Boy's Frosted Grapes

In "The Poor Boy in the Grave"—a cautionary tale about the duties of the wealthy to the poor—an orphan boy is sent to live with a wealthy farmer and his wife, who treat him abominably, giving him little to eat or drink and beating him for the slightest mishap. One day the rich man sets him the errand of taking some bunches of grapes to the local judge. The boy is so hungry and thirsty that he eats two of the bunches along the way. The judge, instead of being angry, sends the boy back to the rich man with the strict instruction that he be better treated.

The beatings continue, however, and one day the boy decides to take his own life. He steals one pot of poison from under the woman's bed, only to discover it is honey, and another pot of poison from the man, which turns out to be wine. Having consumed them, the boy lies down in a freshly dug grave in the churchyard where, overcome by the sudden richness of his diet, he dies, believing he has gone to heaven. Soon after, the rich man loses his house in a fire, and he and his wife spend the rest of their lives in poverty.

Put an artfully arranged plate of these in the center of the table with after-dinner coffee and wait for the gasps of appreciation. Stunning but easy to make, they also look amazing as decoration for a cheesecake or pavlova.

Serves 6–8

Preparation time 20 minutes, plus setting

½ bunch of green seedless grapes

½ bunch of red seedless grapes

a few physalis (optional), with some leaves left intact

1 cup confectioners' sugar

4–5 teaspoons orange or lime juice

¼ cup superfine sugar

1. Wash the grapes and the physalis, if using, then pat dry with paper towels. Snip the grapes into tiny bunches of two or three grapes.

2. Sift the confectioners' sugar into a bowl, then gradually mix in the fruit juice to make a smooth, thick frosting.

3. Dip the grapes a bunch at a time into the frosting, then dip the physalis. Arrange the grapes and physalis on a wire rack set over a cookie sheet. Leave in a cool place for 1 hour or until hardened. Sprinkle with superfine sugar before serving.

The Brothers Grimm Cookbook

On the way, hunger and thirst plagued the lad so much that he ate two of the grape bunches. So when he took the basket to the judge, and the latter had read the letter and counted the grapes, he said, "Two bunches are missing." The boy then honestly confessed, that, driven by hunger and thirst, he had eaten two bunches.

The Poor Boy in the Grave

Frau Holle's Cidered Apple Gelatin

Mother Holle is a kindly being who appears in the Brothers Grimm story named after her, which appeared in the first edition of the *Tales* published in 1812 (in later editions, the tale is named "Old Mother Frost"). In the tale, a young maiden loses her spindle as she sits spinning by a well and jumps down after it. She suddenly finds herself in magical, surreal country. First, she comes across an oven, where some loaves ask to be taken out to stop them from burning, and then an apple tree, which asks her to harvest its fruits. In both instances, the heroine gladly complies. Finally, she comes across a cottage, whose occupant, Mother Holle, invites her to stay in return for a few household chores.

These refreshing desserts might be something kindly Mother Holle would have made for her guest when she turned up at her door, her apron laden with apples.

Your inner child will love these boozy desserts, served daintily in teacups, and they're a great make-ahead option when entertaining.

Serves 6

Prep + cook time 40 minutes, plus chilling

10 cups cooking apples, peeled, cored, and sliced

1¼ cups cider

⅔ cup water, plus 4 tablespoons

⅓ cup superfine sugar

finely grated zest of 2 lemons

4 teaspoons powdered gelatin

½ cup heavy cream

1. Put the apples, cider, the ⅔ cup of measured water, sugar, and the zest of one of the lemons into a saucepan. Cover and simmer for 15 minutes until the apples are soft.

2. Meanwhile, put the 4 tablespoons of water into a small bowl and sprinkle over the gelatin, making sure that all the powder is absorbed by the water. Set aside.

3. Add the gelatin to the hot apples and stir until completely dissolved. Puree the apple mixture in a blender or food processor until smooth, then pour into six teacups. Allow to cool, then chill for 4–5 hours until fully set.

4. When ready to serve, whip the cream until it forms soft peaks. Spoon over the gelatin and sprinkle with the remaining lemon zest.

"Shake us, shake us; we apples are all ripe!"
So she shook the tree till the apples fell down
like rain, and, when none were left on, she
gathered them all together in a heap, and
went further.

Mother Holle (or Old Mother Frost)

"Star Money" Brioche Pudding with Ice Cream

For all their love of the dark and the macabre, the Grimms also had a strong sentimental streak, underpinned by their pious Christian beliefs. This aspect of their work is clearly to the fore in the simple, short tale known as "The Star Money" (or in some editions of the *Tales*, "Star Dollars").

A poor girl has only the clothes she stands up in and a single loaf of bread to keep her from starving. Notwithstanding her poverty, she gives her bread to a hungry beggar and her clothes to three cold children. Now, standing in the darkness in the midst of a forest, she has only her shift and this, too, she gives away to a naked child. At that moment, the stars above the forest canopy fall down about her, transforming into silver coins. Heaven has rewarded her—in quite a literal way—for her virtue and humility.

The girl also finds herself dressed in a new, fine gown. Here we imagine that her loaf of bread has been restored to her, but transformed into the most delicious of fruited brioches. And why not some homemade vanilla and maple ice cream, to boot? Virtue should always get its just desserts—near-pun, of course, intended.

And now she had scarcely anything left to cover herself; and just then some of the stars fell down in the form of silver dollars, and among them she found a petticoat of the finest linen! And in that she collected the star-money which made her rich all the rest of her lifetime!

This is an ideal recipe to use up any leftover Brioche from page 41. Ideal for entertaining, you can make both the ice cream and pudding ahead—it benefits from standing to soak up the cream mixture—and pop it in the oven just before you sit down to eat your main course.

Serves 4

Prep + cook time 1½ hours, plus infusing, cooling, freezing, and soaking

8 slices of brioche

3 eggs, lightly beaten

¼ cup superfine sugar

1 cup milk

⅔ cup heavy cream

½ teaspoon ground mixed spice

2 tablespoons butter, melted

1 tablespoon demerara sugar

For the ice cream

2½ cups heavy cream

1 vanilla pod, split

5 egg yolks

2¾ cups maple syrup

1. First make the ice cream. Put the cream and vanilla pod in a saucepan and heat to boiling point. Remove from the heat and leave to infuse for 20 minutes. Scrape the seeds from the pod into the cream.

2. Beat the egg yolks and maple syrup together in a bowl, stir in the cream, and return to the pan. Heat gently, stirring, until the custard thickens to coat the back of a wooden spoon. Don't allow to boil. Leave to cool. Freeze in a freezerproof container, beating every hour, for 5 hours, or until frozen.

3. Cut the brioche slices diagonally into quarters to form triangles. Arrange, overlapping, in four 8-ounce ramekins.

4. Whisk the eggs, superfine sugar, milk, cream, and spice in a separate bowl. Pour over the brioche slices, pushing them down so that they are almost covered. Drizzle over the butter and sprinkle with the demerara sugar. Leave to soak for 30 minutes.

5. Set the ramekins in a large roasting pan. Pour in enough boiling water to come halfway up the sides of the ramekins. Bake at 350°F for 30 minutes until set and the top is lightly golden. Serve with the ice cream.

Golden Ring Cake

Lost golden rings are an enduring motif in myth and legend. One of the oldest versions is told in *The Histories* of the ancient Greek writer Herodotus, in which Polycrates, the tyrant of Samos in the sixth century BCE, is told to throw away the thing he loves most in order to avoid a reversal of fortune. Polycrates chooses his signet ring and tosses it into the sea. Soon after, the tyrant's cooks prepare a fish for a feast and the ring turns up in its gullet. What in appearance seems to be an astonishing piece of luck in fact seems to suggest that the tyrant's ultimate downfall is unavoidable.

The Grimms' tale "The White Snake" (see page 81 for the full story) has not one but two incidents that seem to echo the ring of Polycrates motif. Near the beginning of the tale a lost golden ring—of whose theft the hero has been accused—turns up in the gullet of a goose, its throat having been sliced open by the king's cook. Then, later, another king tosses a golden ring into the sea as a trial for his daughter's suitors: if the suitor can retrieve the ring, he will marry the princess; if he cannot, he is condemned to drown. The hero, of course, succeeds, retrieving the ring with the help of three friendly fish.

Our cake here is one golden ring that betokens only good fortune . . . and will certainly not miraculously reappear once it has been gobbled down by your appreciative family or guests!

This fruit-packed cake is deliciously moist, thanks to the addition of canned pineapple. For a boozy twist, soak the golden raisins in 2 tablespoons of brandy or rum for at least 30 minutes, preferably 24 hours, beforehand. If you'd rather not cover your cake with icing, try brushing it generously with warmed apricot preserves instead, once it has cooled a little.

Serves 10

Prep + cook time 2 hours, plus cooling

1⅓ cups unsalted butter

⅔ cup superfine sugar

3 large eggs, beaten

3¾ cups self-rising flour, sifted

9 oz. canned pineapple rings in syrup

½ cup candied cherries, chopped

⅔ cup cut mixed peel

3 tablespoons chopped angelica

2 tablespoons chopped walnuts

3 tablespoons dried coconut

½ cup golden raisins

2 tablespoons toasted coconut shavings, to decorate

For the coconut icing

¼ cup unsalted butter

2 cups confectioners' sugar, sifted

2 tablespoons dried coconut

1. Grease a 9-inch ring mold or 8-inch cake pan and line with nonstick baking parchment.

2. Cream the butter and sugar together in a bowl until soft and light, then gradually beat in the eggs. Add the flour and fold into the creamed mixture.

3. Drain the canned pineapple, reserving 1 tablespoon of the syrup for the icing and 3 tablespoons of the syrup for the cake. Chop the pineapple rings finely.

4. Fold the dried fruit, nuts, chopped pineapple, dried coconut, raisins, and the 3 tablespoons syrup into the cake mixture.

5. Pour the mixture into the prepared pan and bake at 325°F for 1¼ hours if using a ring mold, or 1½ hours if using a cake pan. Cool for at least 10 minutes in the pan, then turn out onto a wire rack and leave to cool completely.

6. Once the cake is cool, melt the butter in a saucepan over gentle heat, then take off the heat. Add the confectioners' sugar, remaining pineapple syrup, and the coconut. Stir to combine, then spread the icing over the top of the cake and a little down the sides. Sprinkle with the toasted coconut shavings.

The Woodcutter's Chocolate Log

The forest is one of the archetypal places of the fairy tale. Contrasting with the (relative) security of the village or the palace, it is an untamed wilderness that not only promises adventure and transformation but also threatens disorientation and peril. It is the home of otherworldly beings, a few of whom are undoubtedly good ("The Three Little Men in the Wood," see page 149) but most of whom are untrustworthy or downright evil (the wolf of "Little Red-Cap," for example, or the cannibal-witch of "Hansel and Gretel"—see pages 14 and 35).

The woodcutter, too—living as he does on the edge of the forest and moving between the two worlds—can be an ambivalent, uncanny figure. At one level, the woodcutter must have played a key role in village life, his logs helping to keep people warm and fed. On the other hand, his knowledge of the forest made him a mysterious figure, in touch with dark, otherworldly forces. The character of the woodcutter in "Hansel and Gretel," who, against his better judgment, leads his children deep into the forest, may suggest something of the slippery nature of his profession.

Stray away from the path through the forest and you never know what will happen . . .

The woodcutter in "Hansel and Gretel" ultimately redeems himself, of course. When his children finally return home with treasures, having escaped the wicked witch, he welcomes them with open arms (his new wife has conveniently died). Perhaps he offered his darling offspring a chocolate log just like this one.

The forest seemed to be more and more familiar to them, and at length they saw from afar their father's house. Then they began to run, rushed into the parlor, and threw themselves round their father's neck. The man had not known one happy hour since he had left the children in the forest; the woman, however, was dead. Gretel emptied her pinafore until pearls and precious stones ran about the room, and Hansel threw one handful after another out of his pocket to add to them.

Hansel and Gretel

For a brandy butter version of this log, omit the chestnut and cream filling and instead use 4 oz. of Brandy Butter (see page 50) mixed with ⅔ cup of crème fraîche, and dust the finished cake with cocoa powder instead of confectioners' sugar.

Serves 10

Prep + cook time 1 hour, plus cooling

3 eggs

1¾ cups confectioners' sugar, plus extra for dusting

⅓ cup all-purpose flour, sifted

¼ cup cocoa powder, sifted

1 cup heavy cream

⅔ cup canned sweetened chestnut puree

1⅓ cups plain dark chocolate, broken into pieces

1. Grease a 13 x 9-inch Swiss roll pan and line it with nonstick baking parchment.

2. Whisk the eggs and sugar in a heatproof bowl over a pan of hot water until the mixture leaves a trail when the whisk is lifted. Add the flour and cocoa powder and fold in.

3. Pour into the prepared pan and spread into the corners. Bake at 350°F for about 15 minutes until just firm. Invert the cake onto a sheet of nonstick baking parchment dusted with confectioners' sugar. Peel away the parchment that lined the pan, then roll the sponge in the fresh parchment and leave to cool.

4. Whip half the cream until soft peaks form, then fold in the chestnut puree. Unroll the sponge and spread the chestnut cream over the top (don't worry if the cake cracks). Roll the cake back into a log shape.

5. Bring the remainder of the cream almost to a boil. Remove from the heat and stir in the chocolate pieces. Leave until melted, then stir until smooth. Allow to cool.

6. Arrange the cake, seam side down, on a serving plate. Lightly whip the chocolate cream, then spread it over the top and sides of the cake, and mark to look like tree bark. Dust with confectioners' sugar just before serving.

Gingerbread House

Did the famous edible house in "Hansel and Gretel" begin the German fashion for building gingerbread houses, especially at Christmas, or did it merely reflect a long-established tradition? Scholars are undecided, but other forms of decorated gingerbread—in German, *lebkuchen*—had certainly been around since medieval times, when ginger was first imported into Europe from the Middle East. In some German cities, gingerbread bakers belonged to their own special guild, there were gingerbread fairs, and richly spiced gingerbread was made into all sorts of shapes, from birds and other animals to musical instruments. Queen Elizabeth I of England, who kept a gingerbread cook, is said to have begun the tradition for gingerbread men, having gingerbread portraits of court and foreign dignitaries served at her feasts.

In their famous tale, the Grimms pay a great deal of attention to their edible cottage, although they do not explicitly mention gingerbread in the original tradition, only cake and sugar. Hansel and Gretel are lost in the forest, almost starving, when they come across a little house built from bread with a roof made of cake. The children, naturally, can't resist taking a bite.

Given the famine with which the story has begun, and the hunger specifically of the children, the house represents a fantasy, even a hallucination, of plenty—a vision of a utopia in which everything is good enough to eat and where no one is in want. Of course, the dream soon turns into a nightmare, and the gingerbread house into a house of horrors—the abode of a cannibal witch.

Despite its dark, not-so-sweet underbelly, "Hansel and Gretel" certainly helped to fuel a fashion for gingerbread houses that has only grown over the decades. Today, London's Museum of Architecture commissions dozens of architects every year to make a Christmas gingerbread city to explore an architectural theme such as eco-housing, while the largest gingerbread display ever made, baked and constructed by Jon Lovitch in 2017, encompassed 1,215 buildings.

Now that would have kept not only Hansel and Gretel from hunger but the whole of their village, too. Can I cut you a little bit of window or would you prefer a roof tile?

There are two rules for creating this adorable gingerbread house: one, chill the dough well otherwise the pieces to construct the house will lose their shape and it won't stay up. Two, have as much fun as you can decorating it as lavishly as you like!

Serves 10

Prep + cook time 1 hour, 20 minutes plus chilling, cooling, and setting

½ cup runny honey

¼ cup black molasses

¼ cup unsalted butter, plus extra for greasing

5½ cups all-purpose flour, plus extra for dusting

1½ teaspoons baking soda

1 tablespoon ground ginger

1 egg

2 egg yolks

For the royal icing

2 egg whites

¼ teaspoon lemon juice

3½ cups confectioners' sugar, sifted

1 teaspoon glycerin

1. Heat the honey, molasses, and butter in a saucepan over gentle heat until the butter melts.

2. Add the flour, baking soda, and ginger to a bowl. Add the egg and yolks to the melted butter mixture, then pour over the dry ingredients and mix to a dough. Wrap in plastic wrap and chill for 30 minutes.

3. Roll out the dough on a floured surface and cut out two rectangles, 6 x 4½ inches, for the roof. Cut out two rectangles, 5½ x 3½ inches, for the sides and two squares, 5½ inches, for the ends. Trim each end piece into a triangle point running from the center of the top side to halfway down two opposite sides. Cut holes for doors and windows. From the trimmings, make a door.

4. Place on greased cookie sheets. Bake at 350°F for 10–15 minutes until browning around the edges. Transfer to a wire rack to cool.

To decorate

9 oz. store-bought icing

confectioners' sugar, for dusting

5. Meanwhile, make the royal icing. Place the egg whites and lemon juice in a clean bowl. Using a wooden spoon, stir to break up the egg whites. Slowly add confectioners' sugar, mixing, until the mixture is the consistency of light cream. Continue slowly adding confectioners' sugar in small quantities, stirring all the time. Add the glycerin and mix well.

6. Cover the bowl with damp plastic wrap, sealing well to exclude all air, then set aside to stand so air bubbles can rise to the surface and burst. Stir thoroughly to disperse any air bubbles before using.

7. Spoon royal icing into a piping bag with a writing nozzle. Spread more icing over a silver cake board. Secure the walls of the cottage to the board, gluing sections together with icing. Spread the top edges with icing and secure the roof. Leave for 2 hours to set.

8. Pipe royal icing over the roof sections in any pattern you wish, adding icicles at the roof edges. Then attach and decorate the door.

9. Finish by lightly dusting the house and board with icing sugar, if you wish.

Hansel thought the roof tasted very nice, and so he tore off a great piece; while Gretel broke a large round pane out of the window, and sat down quite contentedly.

Hansel and Gretel

Index

Picture Acknowledgments

Dreamstime.com: Maglara front
cover, 3; Michael Flippo front
cover, 3; Slava296 back cover, 173.
iStock: JulijaDmitrijeva 52. Octopus
Publishing Group: Stephen Conroy
back cover, 31, 65; Will Heap back
cover, 19, 21, 25, 59, 67, 79, 107, 132;
Jonathan Kennedy 139; Louise Lister
153; Lis Parsons 27, 51, 74, 83, 111,
115, 125, 140, 159, 165, 169; William
Reavell 71, 85, 121; William Shaw 11,
15, 29, 47, 92, 101, 105, 116, 119; Ian
Wallace 43, 156, 162.